OAXA

THE ARCHAEO

by Marcus Winter

drawings by
Alberto Beltrán

GLYPH D, in Alfonso Caso's classification, is one of the most widespread symbols in Urban stage Oaxaca, yet it is still not well understood. It appears, for example, on a carved shell from the Cañada, on carved stones at Monte Albán and other Valley of Oaxaca sites, on a stone slab from the District of Choapan, and on a carved human mandible from Eloxochitlán in the Mazatec region.

Although sometimes called a flower, the glyph may be a stylized broad-leafed maguey plant with the dot representing the cavity from which the sap is collected. Or it may represent an ear of corn with leaves. Glyph D sometimes functioned as a day sign in the calendar but occurs in wider contexts which suggests additional meanings and functions; perhaps it symbolized a season of the year.

TITLES IN THE MINUTIAE MEXICANA SERIES

A Flower Lover's Guide to Mexico
A Bird Watcher's Guide to Mexico
A Guide to Mexican Mammals & Reptiles
A Guide to Mexican Archaeology
A Guide to Mexican Witchcraft
A Guide to Mexican History
A Guide to Tequila, Mezcal and Pulque
A Guide to Mexican Poetry, Ancient and Modern
A Guide to Architecture in Ancient Mexico
A Guide to Mexican Ceramics
Minute Guide to Speaking Spanish
Memories of Mexico and Recipes, Too

INDIAN PEOPLES OF MEXICO SERIES

The Maya World
The Aztecs Then and Now
The Great Temple and The Aztec Gods
Oaxaca, the Archaeological Record

Derechos reservados conforme a la ley © 1989.

ISBN 968-7074-21-3
first reprinting, June, 1990

Editorial MINUTIAE MEXICANA, S. A. de C. V.
Insurgentes Centro 114-210; 06030 México, D. F.;
Tel. 535-9488

*There are many representations of Quetzalcoatl, a god
ancient in Middle America before the Christian era
began. We have adopted as the insignia of our series
the most common — that of the feathered serpent. The father
and creator of man, Quetzalcoatl was the beneficent god of life
and the wind, the god of civilization who inspired man to
study the stars, to develop agriculture, industry and the arts.*

Impreso y hecho en México

TABLE OF CONTENTS

KNOWLEDGEMENTS: The author is especially grateful to Nancy Miller
skillful editorial assistance as well as for suggestions about organization of
text. He also thanks Phillips B. Freer and Gibson Winter for comments on
earlier version of the manuscript, Damon Peeler for help with understanding
archaeoastronomy of Oaxaca, and Javier Urcid for clarifying various aspects
Zapotec writing. This book is dedicated to the author's wife Cicely.

photos by the author except pp. 44, 55, 100 (Alfonso Medina) and pp. 76,
, 120 (Anne V. Stenzel).

VER: The panoramic view of Monte Albán is accompanied clockwise, start-
from above, by notable pieces found throughout Oaxaca. The *iguana man*
arently represents an anthropomorphized iguana, resting on his cot. Pottery
rine from Cerro de la Cruz in the Lower Río Verde region of the Oaxaca
st (Urban stage). *Two vessels* from Cueva de Tenango in the Mazatec region
orthern Oaxaca. The small dotted circle on the edge of one design may
esent a hallucinogenic mushroom, used in ceremonies today and in pre-
anic times (City-State stage). An elaborate *Ñuiñe urn* from Tomb 5, Cerro
las Minas in the Mixteca Baja, found between the door jambs at the feet
he principal individual buried in the tomb. The urn is decorated with black,
yellow, and green paint (Late Urban stage). BACK COVER: Urn, man-
odile from the Valley of Oaxaca (Early Urban).

3

INTRODUCTION

Large-scale excavations at Cerro de las Minas
Mixteca Baja began in 1987. Right, work p
in Area G where, in Tomb 5, the Ñuiñe urn
on the cover was found in late 1988.

Ten thousand years ago, perhaps even earlier, a small group
nomadic hunter-gatherers arrived by foot, without beasts of burd
in what is now the state of Oaxaca in southern Mexico. These ea
inhabitants — probably no more than a few families — hunted anim
with stone-tipped spears and foraged for wild plant foods. During su
sequent millenia population increased and many innovations in cult
and society appeared: domesticated plants, complex social and politi
systems, writing, and large urban settlements with monumental arc
tecture.

By A.D. 1200, city-states or kingdoms, each composed of a f
thousand people, existed throughout Oaxaca. Leaders lived in pala
constructed of stone. Craftsmen produced exquisite polychrome potte
High status individuals obtained ornaments and tools of gold, silv
and copper through exchange, and the histories of elite families w
recorded in pictographs in finely painted screen-fold books.

Then in 1519 the Spanish conquerors arrived in what is now Mexi
Within a few years they subjugated most of Mexico's indigenous grou
and introduced new economic, social, and religious systems. Technica
the pre-Hispanic era had ended. Yet in Oaxaca native languages, c
toms, and beliefs have persisted, and are present today.

Based on archaeological evidence this book tells the story of hum
life in Oaxaca from the time of those first arrivals to the coming of
Spaniards. It looks at how and why cultures and societies in Oaxa
changed and how they contributed to the formation of ancient Mes
american civilization. It traces the pre-Hispanic roots of the Zapote
Mixtecs, Chinantecs, Cuicatecs, and many other groups who still inha
Oaxaca and who continue to play a role in the evolution of the sta
and the Mexican nation.

STUDYING PRE-HISPANIC OAXACA

The early immigrants to the New World crossed the Bering Stra
from Asia and spread through North America into Mexico and Cent
America. Physically they were *Homo sapiens sapiens,* that is, they we
the same species as modern man, not some primitive ancestor.

Our knowledge of the origins and developments of the indigenc
groups of Oaxaca is a result of cumulative archaeological resear
Archaeological investigation is relatively young in Oaxaca; many pa

4

the state are undocumented; much work remains to be done, and future studies will alter our perspectives and understanding of the past. Thus it is appropriate to begin our examination of Oaxaca's pre-Historic peoples and cultures with a brief history of how the archaeological record in Oaxaca has been brought to light.

The earliest references to Oaxaca's ancient cities appear in the colonial period when a few authors mention the presence of ancient buildings. For example, the Spanish priest Toribio de Motolinia wrote of the buildings he saw at Mitla during his visit there in 1533 and Alonso de Canseco, author of the 1580 *Relación Geográfica* of Tlacolula and Mitla, described what is now known as the Group of the Columns in Mitla.

Other early visitors to Mexico realized that some tombs and ruins contained gold and other valuables and began the looting and destruction of archaeological sites. In contrast, most indigenous groups during colonial times continued to revere the ancient sites as sacred places and the homes of their ancestors.

The attitudes of non-Indians changed, however, and beginning in the early nineteenth century a genuine historical interest in ancient sites emerged. Local citizens, travelers, antiquarians, and archaeologists wrote about sites in Oaxaca, particularly Monte Albán and Mitla. Some produced scientific papers, supplementing their descriptions with measurements, photographs, and drawings.

An early figure in Oaxaca archaeology was Guillermo Dupaix, commissioned by Spanish monarch Charles IV to inventory the ancient ruins

of New Spain; Dupaix visited Monte Albán in 1806 and uncove
part of the Danzantes Wall. E. A. E. Mühlenpfordt, a German rc
construction engineer, made detailed drawings of the buildings at Mi
in the 1830s. U. S. archaeologist William H. Holmes studied Mi
and Monte Albán in the 1890s, and his analysis of the stone quarr
and construction techniques at Mitla remains the definitive work
those topics.

In the early 1900s Leopoldo Batres, Inspector of Archaeologi
Monuments for the Mexican government, excavated at Mitla and Mo
Albán. He also did some reconstruction at Mitla and moved some
Monte Albán's carved stones to the Museum of Anthropology in Mex
City for display. Around the turn of the century another Germ
Eduard Seler, visited Mitla, Guiengola, and other sites and later p
lished valuable descriptions and illustrations. Yet another early arch
ologist in Oaxaca was Marshall H. Saville of the American Museum
Natural History in New York who excavated at Cuilapan, Xoxocot
and near Mitla in the early 1900s.

The modern era in Oaxaca archaeology began with the research
Alfonso Caso, the brilliant Mexican archaeologist. Caso's book *l*
estelas zapotecas appeared in 1928, and in 1931 he began a long te
program of excavation at Monte Albán in the Valley of Oaxaca. For
first time a detailed and well documented corpus of data on anci
Zapotec culture including carved stone monuments, tombs, architectu
and pottery was brought to light.

In the first season of Caso's excavations at Monte Albán, the sp
tacular Tomb 7 was discovered. The magnificent treasure of gold a
silver ornaments, elaborately carved bones, and numerous other obje
received wide publicity and provided great impetus for continuing
explorations.

To put Monte Albán in a broader context, Caso and his associa
also excavated at Mitla in the Valley of Oaxaca and at several sites
the Mixteca Alta region — Chachoapan, Yucuñudahui, Monte Neg
and Tilantongo. Caso also studied pre-Conquest picture manuscri
and showed that several of these codices deal with places, persons, a
events in the Mixteca Alta.

Four archaeologists who had worked and/or studied with Caso
Ignacio Bernal, Jorge R. Acosta, John Paddock, and Roberto Galle
— continued research on Zapotec and Mixtec cultures. In the Valley
Oaxaca they excavated the sites that are now open to the public: Acc
continued work at Monte Albán; Bernal and Paddock explored Yaj
Bernal excavated Dainzú; Paddock worked at Lambityeco, and Galle
discovered Tombs 1 and 2 at Zaachila. In the Mixteca Alta, Ber
worked at Inguiteria near Coixtlahuaca and Paddock excavated
Yatachio near Tamazulapan.

Thus within a few years Caso and his collaborators and stude
firmly established Oaxaca as a major center of ancient Mexican civ
zation, and their extensive publications made the information availa

Gold pectoral, 11.5 cms. in height, from Tomb 7 at Monte Albán represents a personage wearing a jaguar or serpent headdress, and a human mandible over his jaw. Glyphs on the lower panels represent calendrical year and day signs. Weighing 111.9 grams or 3.91 ounces, it is exquisitely crafted and technically sophisticated, having been poured as one piece.

people throughout the world. However, they offered a vision of pre-Hispanic Oaxaca synonymous with ancient Zapotec and Mixtec cultures alone. Zapotec culture was portrayed as the earlier development followed, after the demise of Monte Albán, by the flowering of Mixtec culture, characterized by codices and high quality craftsmanship in metallurgy and ceramics. This view is understandable given the spectacular nature of Zapotec and Mixtec sites and artifacts, and the fact that most excavations in Oaxaca had been concentrated in the Zapotec and Mixtec regions. However, it was as if other groups in Oaxaca had no distinctive pre-Hispanic origins or developments.

Actually, a few other regions of the state were studied from the 1950s on, but although the results hinted at the cultural complexity and variability of pre-Hispanic Oaxaca, it was rarely clear how developments in these disparate regions might have related to wider cultural patterns in Oaxaca and Mesoamerica. Donald L. Brockington worked around Miahuatlán and along the Pacific Coast between Salina Cruz and the Guerrero border. Several archaeologists worked in the Isthmus: Agustín Delgado around Juchitán; Matthew Wallrath at Tehuantepec; David A. Peterson at Guiengola, and Enrique Méndez in the Huave area. Elsewhere in the state Eduardo Pareyon explored the site of Quiotepec in the Cañada, Howard F. Cline and Delgado worked in the lower Chinantla, Paddock salvaged a tomb at Cerro de las Minas in Huajuapan, and Ronald Spores studied the Nochixtlán Valley. These projects usually involved only minor excavations and surface survey to locate sites.

A major shift in Oaxaca archaeology began in the mid-1960s with research in the Valley of Oaxaca by Kent V. Flannery and his associates and students. Cultural evolution was emphasized, especially from the standpoint of subsistence practices and socio-economic organization.

They applied several innovative approaches that shed new light on pre-Hispanic Oaxaca. One was a concern with human ecology — the study of human occupations within the context of land, water, and

7

other resources, both today and in the past. Also, for the first time Oaxaca, they carried out a region wide, intensive settlement surve This allowed study of pre-Hispanic demography, that is, how populatie grew and communities changed in relation to natural resources and t human environment. A third innovation was the archaeological stue of household organization and domestic economy.

In terms of substantive contributions, Flannery and his associat undertook excavations in Pre-ceramic sites which pushed the Oaxa chronological sequence back in time to many thousands of years befo Christ. They also discovered direct antecedents of Monte Albán throuş excavations in early village sites.

Other research at the same time in regions of the state outside t Valley of Oaxaca had an orientation similar to that of the work ' Flannery and associates. Some examples are Robert and Judith Zeitlir survey and excavations near Juchitan; the survey and excavation the Cañada by Charles Spencer and Elsa Redmond; Charles Markmar survey at Miahuatlan; and work by Spores and Michael D. Lind in t Nochixtlan Valley and by Bruce E. Byland in the Tamazulapan Vall of the Mixteca Alta.

A significant development in Oaxaca archaeology was the creatie in late 1972 of the Centro Regional de Oaxaca, a local office of t INAH or Instituto Nacional de Antropología e Historia (Natior Institute of Anthropology and History), with resident archaeologie as well as specialists in the fields of social anthropology, ethnohistoi and colonial architecture. Staff members of the Center's Archaeolo Section carry out research, protect and maintain sites open to the publ and make information and discoveries known through museums, cc ferences, and publications.

The establishment of this office meant for the first time the sustaine presence of professionally trained archaeologists in Oaxaca. Resear in the initial years included excavations in a residential area of Moi Albán and projects in the Mixteca Alta and the Cañada. Salvage opei tions, recording of accidental discoveries, and brief surveys continue be carried out in many regions, contributing to the emergence of comprehensive view of pre-Hispanic Oaxaca.

In summary, most of the information on archaeology in Oaxaca h been collected in the past 50 years. The chronological sequence is ge erally clear and research has now been done in several regions of t state. But the Zapotec and Mixtec cultures have received disprope tionate attention because the Valley of Oaxaca and the Mixteca regic offer large, important sites more accessible than those of many otl areas.

What follows is an attempt at a general picture of Oaxaca archi ology as it is understood today. We will try to show how cultural develc ments occurred and how the various regions were interrelated. Befc looking at the archaeological record, however, we need to have idea of the setting in which it developed.

Not all Oaxaca is mountainous; there is some flat land, especially on the Isthmus. This view is from Guiengola mountain looking south to the Pacific Ocean. The Tehuantepec river is at the left.

Oaxaca, like many areas of Mexico, is physiographically diverse. ʼo of the earth's crustal plates — the Cocos Plate and the North ᴉerican Plate — meet along the west coast of Mexico so the land continually modified by earthquakes, uplifting, and then erosion. mplementing physiographic diversity is the relatively mild climate ᴉch conditions the agricultural cycle and the types of dwellings people ᴇ.

At 17° north of the equator, Oaxaca is in the tropics at about the ᴉe latitude as southern India, Thailand, the Philippines, and Central rica. Where the land is close to sea level, the climate is hot; it may hot, dry, and desert-like as along parts of the Pacific Coast, or hot ᴉ humid as in the cloud forests and jungles of the northern mountains ᴉ river valleys facing the Gulf of Mexico. Yet much of the state has a ᴉperate climate, being largely highland valleys of 1500 to 2000 ᴇers (5000 to 6500 feet) above sea level. These valleys, in turn, ᴇ surrounded by pine and oak-forested mountains reaching to 3000 more meters (10,000 feet and up).

The year is divided by marked wet and dry seasons. From May ough October, rainy season *(temporal)* crops are grown in valleys ᴉ on hillslopes. During the dry season, from late October through ·ril, cultivation is limited to humid valley bottom lands unless irriga- ᴉ is used.

Oaxaca's great environmental diversity contributed to the emergence cultural and linguistic plurality. At the time of the Spanish conquest ᴇre were at least 16 distinct ethnic and linguistic groups in Oaxaca, ᴉ they are still present today.

Tourists are often told that Oaxaca consists of seven regions: the ᴉley of Oaxaca (or Central Valleys), the Mixteca (Alta and Baja), Coast, the Sierra, the Isthmus, the Cañada, and the Tuxtepec or ᴈaloapan region. Bronze statues of women in native dress from these ᴀs highlight the Fountain of the Seven Regions in Oaxaca City.

However, this division is oversimplified since some of the regions incl
several ethnic and linguistic groups as well as more than one geograp
area.

For our purposes, a finer division includes the following ma
geographic provinces.

The *Valley of Oaxaca* in the center of the state is the largest a
of flat land in highland Oaxaca. Monte Albán and Mitla are loca
here as is the present-day capital, Oaxaca City. The Valley is divi
into sub-areas — the Etla valley, the Tlacolula valley, the Zimatlán
Southern valley, the Ocotlán and Ejutla areas, and the Miahuat
valley.

The *Mixteca Alta* (High Mixteca), a high mountainous region w
of the Valley of Oaxaca, broken into numerous small intermont
valleys, including the Nochixtlán Valley, scene of much archaeolog
work.

The *Mixteca Baja* (Low Mixteca), also a mountainous area
lower, hotter, and more arid and rocky than the Alta, in the west
part of Oaxaca and continuing into the state of Guerrero. It is a
divided into many small valleys.

The *Mixteca de la Costa* (Coast Mixteca), a relatively low, h
area in the southwest corner of the state including the western e
of the coast. A hot and arid region.

The *Coast* is the southern strip of the state bordering the Pac
Ocean; generally a hot, dry region cut by large rivers that originate
the highlands.

The *Isthmus* (of Tehuantepec) includes the extensive coastal pl
and low mountains between Tehuantepec and Coatzacoalcos, Verac

The *southern mountains* comprise a poorly defined area betw
the coast to the south and the Valley of Oaxaca and the Mixteca /
to the north.

The *Chimalapas* in the extreme eastern part of Oaxaca is a mo
tainous area bordered on the north by the state of Veracruz, on
east by the state of Chiapas, and on the south by a narrow coa
plain and the Pacific Ocean.

The *Mixe region* includes the mountains east and northeast of
Valley of Oaxaca and some low river valleys bordering on the Isthm

The *Zapotec Sierra* or Sierra Juárez is the mountain range n
of the Valley of Oaxaca.

The *Chinantla* includes mountains of the northern extreme of
Zapotec Sierra as well as the river valleys and piedmont sloping d
to the Gulf Coast of Veracruz.

The *Mazatec region* includes the highland and piedmont river val
just to the northwest of the Chinantla.

To the west of the Mazatec region in the northwest corner of Oax
are the mountains which form part of a chain oriented northwest-so
east extending into Puebla and Veracruz states. This region is curre
occupied by Nahuatl speakers.

10

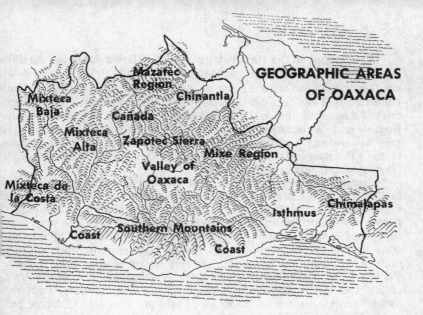

GEOGRAPHIC AREAS OF OAXACA

The *Cañada* is the deep canyon, including the mountain sides defin-
it, between the Mixteca Alta on the west and the Mazatec and
otec regions to the east.

Sometimes the archaeological information presented here is orga-
ed in terms of these divisions but the reader should bear in mind
t there is no necessary correlation between geographic provinces and
nic or linguistic groups. In fact, it is common to find that a particular
up occupies several distinct ecological zones which may extend into
erent geographical regions. This gives the group access to a variety
environments, resources, and products. Thus the geographic distri-
ion of archaeologically documented groups cannot be assumed but
st be determined through the distribution of similar artifacts and
tural patterns.

The distinction "highland-lowland" appears occasionally in the
t and refers simply to mountainous versus flat-coastal and relatively
land nearly at sea level. Most of Oaxaca is highlands but lowlands
ur in the Isthmus, along the Pacific Coast, and in the extreme north
the state in river valleys bordering Veracruz.

TURAL AND LINGUISTIC DIVERSITY

Oaxaca's rugged and varied terrain has contributed to spatial separa-
of human populations, permitting diversity to flourish and a mosaic
ethnic and linguistic groups to emerge. To some extent, ethnic groups
Oaxaca have distinct patterns of economic, social, and religious-cere-
nial life, although these patterns are sometimes blurred among groups.
contrast, language is easier to objectify and thus serves as a clear
erion to distinguish groups.

Most groups in the state belong to two different language families the Otomangue family and the Mixezoque family. Three other famil are represented in Oaxaca, each by a single language. Language famil (named for their northern and southernmost members) are groups related languages, that is, languages with a common origin. For examp English and German are members of the same family though of cou they are distinct and not mutually intelligible. Similarly, the langua; in the Otomangue family have common roots but are totally differe languages and not simply dialects.

Linguistic data complement and amplify the archaeological reco in Oaxaca. The distribution of linguistic groups in Oaxaca today p vides a starting point for determining their distribution in the past. T present-day distribution corresponds closely to that in late pre-Hispa; times and in the Colonial period just after the Conquest. This is kno from historical documents and from late communities observa' archaeologically. For example, we can be quite sure that the site Pueblo Viejo in Cuicatlán was originally inhabited principally by C catecs and that the material remains — houses, pottery, implemer and so forth — are manifestations of late pre-Hispanic Cuicatec cult in the Cañada.

By studying late pre-Hispanic communities in areas where we kn what language was spoken, we can establish possible correlations archaeological remains with linguistic groups. However, as we go f ther back in time, not centuries but millenia, archaeological rema become relatively scarce and poorly preserved. Temporal continu with the present is interrupted.

At this point a specialty within linguistics comes into play, name linguistic prehistory, which is the study of origins, changes, and div sification of distinct languages. Linguistic prehistory is useful for traci the emergence of pre-Hispanic groups in Oaxaca. Linguists have dev oped a technique called glottochronology for comparing related la guages and determining how many centuries have passed, at a minimu since the languages separated from each other or from a comm ancestor.

MESOAMERICA
OAXACA

Although Oaxaca covered a relatively small portion of the overall area of Meso-america's high cultures, it was the site of the first great city (Monte Albán) and two of the Mesoamerican written languages (Zapotec and Mixtec).

MEXICO CITY

GUATEMALA CITY

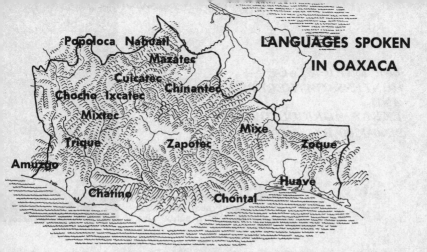

LANGUAGES SPOKEN IN OAXACA

even languages spoken in Oaxaca (Amuzgo, Chatino, Zapotec, Chinantec,
ocho, Ixcatec, Mazatec, Popoloco, Cuicatec, Mixtec, and Trique) belong to
Otomangue family. Two, Mixe and Zoque, make up the Mixe-Zoque family,
d three (Chontal, Nahuatl and Huave) are single representatives of their
milies. The Otomangue languages are tonal; the meaning of a word may
pend on the register in which it is pronounced.

VERSITY AND UNITY

Pre-Hispanic groups in Oaxaca did not develop in isolation: they
changed raw materials, finished products, techniques, and ideas with
ighboring groups, and they also participated in wider changes in
esoamerica though trade and other interaction. And, Oaxaca is
uated in the center of Mesoamerica, the geographic area from central
exico to Costa Rica in Central America where the ancient high
ilizations arose.

In broad terms, Mesoamerica can be divided into five areas: Central
exico, Western Mexico, the Gulf Coast, Oaxaca, and the Maya region.
rticularly important in relation to Oaxaca are the major centers of
e-Hispanic groups northwest of Oaxaca, including the Tehuacán
lley, the Puebla-Tlaxcala area, and the Basin of Mexico. (The great
ies of Teotihuacan, Tula, and the Aztec capital of Tenochtitlan were
ated in the Basin of Mexico.) To the north of Oaxaca is Veracruz
d the Gulf Coast, best known as the heartland of Olmec culture. The
aya flourished to the east of Oaxaca in Chiapas, the Yucatán penin-
la, Guatemala, and beyond.

Trade and interaction with groups in these other areas counter-
lanced the cultural diversity engendered by geographic separation
pre-Hispanic Oaxaca. Hence an interplay of two trends — diversity
the emergence of culturally and linguistically distinct groups, and
ity through interaction and communication among the groups —
rmed the peoples and cultures of ancient Oaxaca. In the chapters
t follow, we will see how these complementary trends worked in the
mation of the archaeological record.

THE LITHIC STAGE - -
HUNTERS, GATHERERS,
AND
EARLY AGRICULTURISTS:
9500-1500 B.C.

Chipped stone projectile point found near San Juan Guelavía, shown actual size.

The pre-Hispanic occupation of Oaxaca begins with the Litl stage, also known as the Pre-ceramic, so designated because stone to are the most common preserved artifacts, and ceramics were abse Probably 200 to 300 people at most lived in Oaxaca during this sta a population consisting of small nomadic groups who subsisted collecting wild plant foods and hunting and trapping animals. Th also took the first steps in cultivating plants and initiating th domestication.

The Lithic stage is divided into the Paleo-Indian period, from ab 9500 to 7000 B.C., followed by the Archaic period, from about 70 to 1500 B.C.

THE PALEO-INDIAN PERIOD

The earliest evidence of man's presence in Oaxaca is a chipp stone projectile point found on the surface near the town of San Ju Guelavía in the Tlacolula Valley, about 20 kilometers southeast Oaxaca City. The point was probably lost during a hunting expeditic The distinctive flutes or channels on each surface relate the po stylistically to those used by the Clovis mammoth hunters who lived the western United States between 9500 and 9000 B.C. It is made locally available gray-brown chert, was probably hafted to a wood foreshaft — a short, arrow-like stick — and set into a thicker, heav spear shaft.

Spears were thrown by hand, usually employing a spear thrower a lever. The expendable foreshaft may have stuck in an animal or brok off and been lost if the target was missed, while the spear itself f away and was perhaps recovered.

The makers of the Guelavía projectile point, like the Clovis peop may have hunted big game — mammoths, mastodons, Pleistoce horses, and other extinct fauna (fossil bones of these animals ha been discovered in many regions of Oaxaca though not in associati with man-made artifacts) — as well as hunting and trapping smal animals — deer, antelope, rabbits and birds. Another possible Pale

lian find in Oaxaca consists of burned animal bones found in the
vest level of Cueva Blanca rockshelter near Mitla. Here, too, evidence
man's presence remains ambiguous since no artifacts were found.

E ARCHAIC PERIOD

Around 7000 B.C. the climate in Oaxaca seems to have become
rmer. Vegetation zones appear to have shifted and conditions similar
those of today emerged. In the highland valleys the pine zone moved
higher, steeper slopes; the alluvial areas along the principal rivers
nained forested and the piedmont slopes probably supported open
squite and brush woodlands. Today, of course, the natural vegetation
many parts of Oaxaca has been modified by clearing for planting
ps and cutting of firewood. The valleys and lowlands are now much
re open and subject to erosion.

The demise of the Pleistocene megafauna and the possible shift
a warmer climate would have required a reorientation of subsistence
tterns by hunter-gatherer groups. The people would now have needed
rely on small game and the collection and processing of wild plant
ds. In coastal areas there was probably exploitation of lagoon and
uary resources such as fish, shrimp, and clams, although thus far
Oaxaca, Archaic period remains have been found only in the high-
ds, not in lowland areas.

The best known Archaic sites in southern Mexico are the rock-
elters near Mitla, Oaxaca, and in the Tehuacan Valley, Puebla. These
large overhangs or shallow caves which provided convenient natural
tection from wind, rain, and sun. Occupation layers and artifacts
well preserved in rockshelters but these sites give the erroneous
pression that people lived mainly in caves. In most cases, however,
kshelters were simply temporary camps. The "living floors" rep-
ent long term accumulations of debris rather than single events.
tually, most Archaic period camp sites were in the open; people
de brush and animal skin huts and used cooking hearths and open-
work areas. However, such sites are difficult to recognize archaeo-
ically since most refuse was dispersed and the perishable remains
integrated in time.

The relative abundance of Archaic sites near Mitla may be due
the fact that this is one of the few locales in the Valley of Oaxaca
ere good quality stone for flaked implements can be obtained. For
usands of years, groups and individuals came there to exploit the
ne for at least preliminary roughing out of their tools. A lot of
ris is generated during tool production, especially if it occurs off
l on for thousands of years. If people came to exploit the stone out-
ps for several days at a time, it is logical that they would leave
ains of food collection, preparation, and consumption along with
ir chipping waste. Good quality chert also occurs at Yucuñudahui
the Mixteca Alta, another site with evidence of occupation by
chaic groups.

Archaic period tools were simple. Many were made from perishab[le] materials such as wood and fibers — for example, digging stic[k] tongs for picking cactus fruits, traps, nets, and bags. The rare existi[ng] examples have been found in dry deposits in Guilá Naquitz rockshel[ter] near Mitla; other examples are known from similar sites in the Tehuac[án] Valley, Puebla. Stone tools included grinding implements for processi[ng] wild grain and seeds and chipped-stone projectile points, kniv[es] scrapers, and perforators.

Food Varieties and Sources

Wild plant and animal foods provided the subsistence base f[or] early hunters and gatherers in Oaxaca in both the Paleo-Indian a[nd] Archaic periods. Wild plant foods included cactus fruits, mague[y] *nanches* (a small, tree-borne fruit) and acorns. Two important pla[nt] foods, pine nuts and *teosinte,* the probable ancestor of corn, apparen[tly] occurred here in the wild thousands of years ago but are no long[er] present. Deer, peccary, rabbits, birds, and other small animals we[re] hunted and trapped.

Some plants can be eaten with a minimum of preparation. Oth[ers] such as acorns must be shelled or husked and soaked and/or cooked [in] water and rinsed to remove the bitter taste. Teosinte produces sm[all] triangular seeds with a tough outer coat or shell. The shell provi[des] roughage if it is eaten but it can be removed by grinding with a st[one] and mortar. Inside is the tiny, round nutritious kernel.

Varieties of maguey or agave are still cultivated today in the Mi[tla] area and in the mountains along the highway from Mitla down towa[rd] the Isthmus of Tehuantepec. In pre-Hispanic times the hard tips of [the] long, bayonet-like spikes were used as needles or perforators. W[ith] care they can be pulled off the leaf together with strands of fiber a[s a] ready-made needle and thread. The heart or center of the plant w[ith] the spikes cut off was roasted in a subsurface earth oven to yield [a] juicy, sweet pulp high in carbohydrates. (Today the hearts are boil[ed], fermented, and then distilled to make *mezcal,* Oaxaca's equivalent [of] the tequila of western Mexico.) Maguey worms, reddish, shiny lar[vae] resembling naked caterpillars, are found at the base of the plant. Th[ey] are still considered a delicacy today, rivaling grasshoppers and tu[rkey] eggs as Oaxaca specialties since pre-Hispanic times.

Social Organization

The micro-band/macro-band model of social organization propos[ed] by archaeologist R. S. MacNeish suggests how people may have [or]ganized themselves in order to take advantage of food resources dur[ing] the Archaic period. During most of the year, according to this vie[w] people lived in small groups or micro-bands, probably composed [of] nuclear families or small extended families. They moved from pl[ace] to place seasonally, following available food resources. Periodica[lly] however, several groups may have joined together, forming a mac[ro]

16

nd for the exploitation of abundant resources that could have pro-
ced food for a large group. This might have occurred, for example,
en an extensive stand of teosinte or *guaje* (pods of an acacia tree
ntaining edible seeds) became ripe. But what did the people do with
ese harvests? Abundant stands didn't necessarily occur in places that
d water, shelter, or other features required for life, so some potential
rvests surely went unutilized.

Also, storage and transport must have created problems. There
re no beasts of burden in pre-Hispanic Mexico, and it is unprofitable
transport food over long distances by human back because the carriers
nsume it. There is no evidence of storage facilities from this period.
en after plant cultivation began, people may have dispersed during
ner times of the year, then coalesced for harvest. Hunting and trap-
ng were probably done throughout the year.

rly Agriculture and Plant Domestication

The beginning of agriculture and domestication of plants was the
st important cultural development of the Lithic stage in Mesoamerica.
xaca was one of the areas that played a role in this change.

Literally dozens of native Mexican plants presumably provided food
' hunter-gatherers during the Lithic stage. Some, such as acorns, wild
ions, field greens, and fruits such as nanches and hackberries, were
ver domesticated although they figured in the diet and in some cases
still important today. A second group — *nopal* or prickly pear
ctus (both the leaves and the fruits, or *tunas,* are eaten), amaranth,
guey, zapotes and others — were collected in the wild and probably
tivated at times, as they are today. Both these groups have remained
rphologically about the same over thousands of years. A third group
sists of plants initially collected in the wild and cultivated from
ly times that eventually underwent significant genetic changes making
m more productive from a human standpoint. These plants — corn,
ans, squash, chiles, and avocados — have been the mainstays of the
soamerican diet for thousands of years.

The full story of where, why, and how early agriculture and plant
mestication took place in Mesoamerica has yet to be unfolded.
rieties of squash and beans dated to 8000 B.C. have been found in
ckshelters in Tamaulipas, the Tehuacán Valley in Puebla, and the
lley of Oaxaca. Evidence of domesticated plants appears in sub-
quent millenia: cucurbits (squash) in Guilá Naquitz in Oaxaca
und 7000 B.C., early corn in the Tehuacán Valley around 5000
C., and beans, also in Tehuacán, between 4000 B.C. and 3000 B.C.

Several theories have been advanced as to why domestication oc-
rred. Some have argued that climatic change forced, or at least stim-
ted, groups to develop alternative food sources. Others have said
t agriculture was developed in response to growing populations.
ither of these arguments is acceptable, however. First, there is no
dence of radical climatic change during the Archaic and, second,

17

as we have already seen, populations were so low that they would ha
been unlikely to put undue pressure on existing resources. Anoth
suggested possibility is that cultivation was initiated to compensa
for irregular harvests of wild plant foods in unusually dry or wet yea

It seems more probable that domestication began as plants we
brought from their original, wild habitats to camp sites occupied
hunter-gatherer groups for other reasons: availability of water, shelt
abundant wild plant foods, good hunting and trapping, and chert o
crops. These places didn't necessarily correspond to the areas whe
the wild ancestors of corn, beans, squash, or other plants grew. Ho
ever, early hunter-gatherers are likely to have had a comprehensi
knowledge of plant distribution and plant behavior, and it would ha
been logical for them to move plants around to places they would
revisiting from year to year. By planting some beans or squash befc
leaving a site, for example, these would have been available perha
for the next year's or the next season's visit. Thus domestication co
well have been part of a process of spatially concentrating resource:

This last hypothesis — the gradual centralization of food sources -
is attractive because it also may account for more productive strains
plants. In moving plants to new habitats it is possible, or even higl
likely, that the largest seeds or most vigorous specimens would ha
been chosen. Farmers in Oaxaca today select the best (i.e., large
healthiest) seeds for next year's planting. If such a process of selecti
went on year after year in Pre-ceramic times, while it would not ha
led to genetic changes, it would at least have led to more producti
varieties because the hunter-gatherers would have been selecting f
better harvests. Genetic changes occur through mutation. If a gro
recognized mutations in plants and selected those seeds for plantir
new strains would have been developed.

We should bear in mind also that cultivation is not the same thi
as domestication. Cultivation — the manipulation of plants to promc
and protect their growth (and including changes of habitat, as me
tioned above) — may have begun from earliest times. But howev
they occurred, the genetic changes leading to greater yield, i.e. domes
cation, were the crucial factor that made greater reliance on cultivat
foods possible.

The Tehuacán Tradition

Archaic occupations in highland Oaxaca were like those to t
northwest in the Tehuacán Valley, the Basin of Mexico, and the sta
of Hidalgo and Querétaro; together they formed what might be call
the Tehuacán Tradition. The same or related groups of people produc
similar archaeological remains in these areas, including projectile poi
of distinctive styles, grinding stones used for processing plant foo
and remains of cultivated plants, indicating incipient agriculture.

The geographical distribution of the Tehuacán Tradition correspor
to the distribution of the Otomangue family of languages in histc

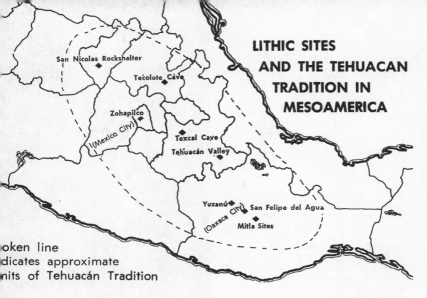

San Nicolas Rockshelter

Tecolote Cave

Zohapilco

(Mexico City)

Texcal Cave

Tehuacán Valley

Yuzanú

San Felipe del Agua

(Oaxaca City)

Mitla Sites

oken line
dicates approximate
nits of Tehuacán Tradition

les. Since the majority of Oaxaca languages today belong to the
omangue family, it is likely that the Pre-ceramic occupants of Oaxaca
re direct ancestors of the Zapotecs, Mixtecs, Chinantecs, and other
oups present there now.

In sum, the Lithic stage is present but still poorly understood as it
isted in Oaxaca. According to linguistic analysis, diversification of
e Otomangue family had begun by 4400 B.C. This diversification
ay have been related to agricultural intensification. Greater depen-
nce on cultivated food could have led to population growth and
creased sedentariness, which in turn could have increased isolation
groups, thus promoting linguistic variation. However, since the
riod from 3000 B.C. to 1500 B.C. is the least well documented of
y Mesoamerican time span, only future research will permit con-
mation of this hypothesis.

It is worth noting that hundreds of Paleo-Indian and Archaic sites
e known in North America while only a handful are reported in
exico. This may be due in part to the greater quantity of archaeo-
gical work done in the United States as compared to Mexico and to
e fact that many more archaeological sites in the United States have
en exposed through large scale construction projects. Further, most
the sites known in Mexico are from piedmont or mountain slopes;
any Archaic camp sites may actually have been in low-lying areas
xt to major rivers and were either washed away by floods or covered
er by alluvium. On the other hand, the scarcity of sites may actually
a valid indicator that the number of people in Mexico during Archaic
nes was quite small. Better documentation and fuller understanding
the Lithic stage are major challenges for future archaeological work
Oaxaca.

THE VILLAGE STAGE:
1500-500 B.C.

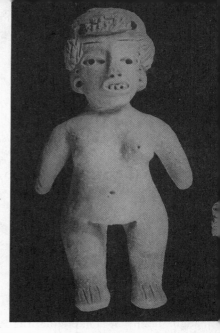

When this female figurine was found, its hollow abdomen was filled with dirt. On cleaning, the baby was discovered within the cavity. The pair, unearthed at the Hacienda Blanca site in the Valley of Oaxaca, date from the Tierras Largas phase. This creation of a pregnant woman with a baby that could be put inside or taken out is a unique piece.

Between 1500 and 1400 B.C., permanent village settlements we established in several regions of Oaxaca. Inhabitants of these sm communities made pottery and cultivated crops. Year round occup tion meant that they could acquire property and goods — a house, la and nonportable tools such as ceramic vessels and heavy stone *mar* and *metates* for grinding corn — and that they could identify with specific place. All of this contrasts with the earlier nomadic way of l which involved a minimum of tools, no permanent shelter, and d ferent concepts of property and territoriality.

The village was the most common and dominant form of settleme in Oaxaca from 1400 to 500 B.C. Villages persisted in later times a are still present today. Many patterns of life in Oaxaca were establish during the Village stage, among them those of food production a consumption, household organization and division of labor, and bur practices. These patterns formed the basis for the emergence of compl society in subsequent periods. Thus the Village stage is sometimes call the Formative period in pre-Hispanic Mesoamerica.

According to linguistic studies, the nine principal branches of t Otomangue language family were formed by 1500 B.C., the peri when sedentary villages appear in several regions of the Otomang area. This suggests that establishment of settled villages may be relat to linguistic diversification: as population increased within a localiz region, mobility and contacts between groups in different regions c creased, thus promoting linguistic diversity.

Early village settlements clustered in areas of prime agricultu land. As population grew, villages flourished and new communit

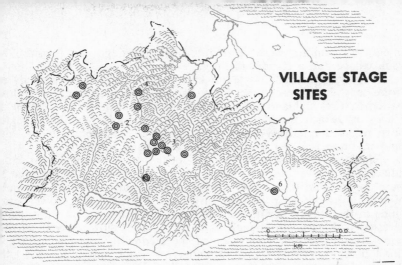

VILLAGE STAGE SITES

Mixteca Baja (Santa Teresa, El Guayabo); 2. Mixteca Alta (Etlatongo, Yu-
ta); 3. Valley of Oaxaca (Abasolo, Fábrica San José, Hacienda Blanca, Huitzo,
la, San José Mogote, Santa María Chichihualtepec, Tierras Largas, Tomal-
ec); 4. Cañada (Hacienda Tecomaxtlahua, Rancho Dolores Ortiz); 5. Chi-
tla (Ayotzintepec); 6. Isthmus (Laguna Zope).

re established five to 10 kilometers apart. Contact among communi-
s within a given valley, for example, promoted formation of common
ltural patterns and shared linguistic elements, but they were distinct
m those in other valleys. In this way separate linguistic and ethnic
ups emerged.

Since, as noted, the period from 3000 to 1500 B.C. is poorly
cumented in Oaxaca and Mesoamerica generally, the origins of per-
nent villages remain unclear. We don't know if hunter-gatherers in
eral regions gradually adopted a sedentary way of life or if im-
grants from other areas established the first villages. Perhaps both
curred. In any case, plant cultivation and food storage, must have
en directly involved in making sedentary life possible.

A reliable subsistence base is a prerequisite for permanent settle-
nt. Since plant domestication and cultivation began by 5000 B.C.
earlier, it was not simply agriculture that marked the change from
madism to permanent settlement. Villagers also must have had a
tritionally adequate combination of productive, high yield plants,
ich included corn, beans, squash, avocado, and others. And they
st have developed food storage methods. Storage capability means
t food can be conserved, that consumption can be delayed and
nned for the future. Underground storage pits represent a techno-
;ical innovation and appear for the first time with the early villages.

Most early villages in Oaxaca consisted of from three to 10 families
households. They were nucleated communities, that is, dwellings
re grouped together rather than dispersed over the landscape as in
er rural settlements. Nucleation implies that the communities were

21

integrated; families were related through marriage and kinship, a each village had a distinct identity.

Early villages in Oaxaca are known both from the highlands a from coastal regions; these form two distinct traditions or cultu patterns. The highland village tradition is known from sites in Valley of Oaxaca, the Mixteca Alta, and the Cañada. Since these regio have received relatively more attention from archaeologists, the hig land tradition is better known than the lowland tradition.

Highland villages were usually located on low piedmont rid, adjacent to a river; they had access to a permanent water source were above flood level. Rich, humid alluvial soils permitted cultivati of two crops per year without irrigation. At 1500 B.C. river botto lands in the Valley of Oaxaca and other highland valleys were heav forested with large trees such as cypress and willow as well as thi underbrush. The thin, rocky soil of the piedmont slopes adjoining flood plain supported scrub vegetation — cacti, mesquite, and oth thorny plants similar to those seen today. Higher up, away from valley floor, were pine and oak zones that provided acorns, wood fuel and house construction, and game such as deer and peccary.

Villagers were faced with the initial task of clearing the for from the alluvium. This was probably done with the same slash-ar burn technique used in many parts of Oaxaca today: brush and tre are cut, left to dry out, and then burned. Stone axe heads, which wo have been hafted to wooden handles, are found commonly in villa sites and must have been the main tool along with fire for cleari land. The initial clearing was a major task and investment of time a energy. Once cleared, alluvial land could be used year after year, w occasional rainy season floods replenishing soil nutrients.

A lowland coastal tradition existed at the same time. Settleme were located next to major rivers on low (sometimes artificial) ri out of flood range. Houses, probably made of sticks with thatch roo were likely to have been cool but less elaborate than the highla wattle-and-daub houses. Food was probably stored in bags and n suspended from the rafters rather than in underground pits. Fish a shellfish gathered from rivers and lagoons supplemented a diet bas on cultivated corn. Spherical ceramic pots with small holes in the t called *tecomates,* were used for cooking. This pre-Hispanic traditi appears in Oaxaca in the Isthmus of Tehuantepec and was apparen associated with Mixezoque speakers who also inhabited parts of coas Veracruz, western Chiapas, and the Pacific coast of Chiapas.

HOUSEHOLDS

The household was the basic social group within the village. Hous holds were small, consisting of a nuclear family (a man, a woman, a their children) of perhaps five members. The household was the bas unit of production and consumption, providing food, shelter, and ca for its members.

Households are evidenced archaeologically by separate clusters of mains that include a house structure, storage pits, ovens, refuse deposits, and burials. By studying these groupings we can see how the households functioned and how they changed through time.

The Village stage household was equivalent to the nuclear family "microband" of the Archaic period. New domestic activities appeared in the Village stage but composition of family groups remained about the same. This is not surprising since the family is a natural group: continuance of the human species through reproduction and nurturing of the offspring takes place in a family setting — a nuclear family of male, female, and children, or an extended family involving additional relatives. Small villages were probably composed of several related families.

Comparison of household remains suggests that the village organization was egalitarian: there appear to have been no great disparities between households in economic, political, or social status. Within the village there was some part-time specialization in production of goods like pottery and woven cloth, and there were undoubtedly cooperative work groups for tasks such as house construction, land clearance, planting, harvesting and hunting.

Houses during the Village stage, at least in the highlands, were rectangular, about five by three meters. They were made with wooden corner posts and wattle-and-daub walls, that is, cane lashed together with fibers and plastered with mud. Stones were placed to form a threshhold at the doorway, and along the base of the walls to prevent erosion. Roofs were thatch — grass or palm bundles tied on a pole frame.

Many household activities were performed in an outside patio next the house. Food was stored in underground pits, sometimes called "bell-shaped pits" because they are wide at the base and narrow at ground level. They ranged in volume from one to four cubic meters. one-cubic meter pit could store enough shelled corn to last a family five for several months.

Ovens of various sizes and forms (circular, oval, rectangular), usually dug below ground level, attest to activities such as pottery firing and steaming or roasting food.

Above, the heavy stone metate and mano were used for crushing corn kernels.

Below, the tecomate was the stew pot of the coastal region.

23

The household was established as the focus of domestic life in the Village stage. Adjacent corn field, storage pit and oven made it an independent unit. The dead were buried nearby, thus continuing as family members.

Refuse was usually discarded near the house in low spots in the ground or in an abandoned pit. These dumps often yield broken pottery, bone and stone tools, as well as food remains such as burned animal bone or carbonized remains of corn cobs and kernels, beans, avocado and other plant foods which give us an idea of the villagers' diet. Corn, beans, and avocados were the major plant foods, supplemented by chiles, *miltomate* (the small, green tomato used commonly today in Oaxaca to make sauces), and squash. Deer, peccary, opossum, rabbit, possibly dog, and various birds were sources of meat.

Much of daily life revolved around obtaining and preparing food. Anyone who observes activities in a Oaxaca village today will notice that these tasks continue to occupy a lot of the work time invested by men, women, and children. Land clearing was only the first step in cultivation. Planting was done with a digging stick to make a hole in the soil into which a few seeds were dropped. Fields had to be weeded occasionally during the three or more months of plant maturation, and then came the harvest and drying of grain before storage.

Three thousand years ago, corn kernels were smaller than those of today. Manos and metates from this period are large and heavy, indicating that a lot of effort was needed to crush the kernels and prepare them for consumption. Women living today in Oaxaca villages without electricity or gasoline driven mills still spend hours each morning grinding corn for the day's tortillas.

Corn was probably eaten in the form of mush or cooked dough, perhaps wrapped in corn husks and steamed like tamales. It also may have been baked into little cakes. The tortilla was "invented" toward the end of the Village stage. We know this because it was during this stage that the clay griddles used for baking them appeared.

The tecomates or cooking vessels of the coastal tradition suggest that in the lowlands food was prepared as a kind of stew or watery soup with many ingredients tossed into the pot and boiled.

Ceramic figurines representing both males and females give us an
ea of the clothing worn by villagers. Men wore loincloths, probably
woven material, and sometimes sandals tied at the ankles and made
fibers or animal hides. Women used cloth or fiber skirts, sometimes
corated with fringes, and sandals as well, and they wore their long
ir braided or twisted in elaborate hairdos. Jewelry included earspools,
cklaces of stone or shell beads, and pendants.

Villagers buried their dead outside their houses in graves or aban-
ned pits. The dead thus remained close to the family as household
embers. Remains are usually found in extended position and accom-
nied by simple offerings of a few ceramic vessels as well as personal
ornments. A jade or greenstone bead was sometimes placed in the
ad person's mouth. This practice, also known in other cultures of
e world, perhaps symbolized perpetual life. (Greenstone is a catchall
rm for metamorphic rock of a greenish color, much more common in
axaca than jade or jadeite.)

RADE

Trade was another important aspect of early village life in Oaxaca.
involved nonlocal materials such as obsidian, shell, greenstone, and
ottery as well as local products including ceramic figurines, salt, and
obably perishable items like wooden poles or masks, and palm mats
d baskets. All households seem to have participated in the trade
etworks through which goods and information were exchanged and
gional ties were developed.

Exactly how trade was carried out in village times remains to be
etermined. We know that as early as 1000 B.C., for example, highland
axaca villagers received obsidian from sources hundreds of kilometers
vay in Veracruz, in Central Mexico, and even Guatemala. Did the
llagers themselves travel to these distant sources? Did foreign traders
ing the obsidian to Oaxaca? Were travelers able to carry provisions
r long distance trips and pass unharmed through territories occupied
y other ethnic and linguistic groups whose customs and language
ey did not share? Perhaps the obsidian was passed from village to
llage, eventually arriving in Oaxaca. (In some cases, distances be-
veen neighboring villages were considerable. For example, commu-
ties in the Etla Valley and the Cañada were separated by two days'
alk, but some kind of contact seems clearly to have existed.) Once
e exotic materials arrived in a valley with several communities, they
uld have been traded among households in exchange for locally
vailable specialized items.

RELIGION AND RITUAL

Ritual and ceremonial activities were important aspects of village
fe in ancient Oaxaca. The yearly agricultural cycle and the human
fe cycle of birth, puberty, marriage, and death are common themes
at structure ritual and ceremony among most peoples. We can infer,

25

though without explicit details, that both public and private rituals and ceremonies took place. Public ceremonies probably occurred at harvest time,[1] involving dances and feasting. Relatively private rituals would have centered around family matters — invocations petitioning fertility, and safe and healthy births; healing ceremonies, and funeral rites.

Ceramic figurines also give some clues to ritual attire. Animals are sometimes represented but most figurines depict human beings — pregnant women with elaborate headdresses, men in seated position, men wearing animal masks. These are self-representations, that is, they show the people themselves. Figurines may have been set up in scenes or arranged so that gods, spirits, or forces could be invoked to aid or propitiate the desires and needs of individuals or the group. Some figurines were probably used in rituals having to do with pregnancy and birth as well as protection of family members.

Designs were painted on the body with clay roller seals, perhaps for rites and ceremonies. Sting ray spines were used in blood-letting ceremonies performed in conjunction with offerings made to the spirits in request for or in return for assistance.

Musical instruments played at ceremonies may also have been children's toys. Small pottery whistles in the shape of birds and animals are found frequently in Valley of Oaxaca villages. They produce two different tones, depending on whether the hole in the hollow body is stopped with a finger or left open. Instruments made of perishable materials, for example, turtle shell drums and rattles of dried squash and gourds, appear to have been common. A spherical ceramic rattle containing tiny pebbles — apparently an imitation gourd rattle — was found at the early village site of Hacienda Blanca in the Etla Valley. Ceramic flutes that produce several tones and drums made from large sea turtles are known from the City-State stage.

Rituals were undoubtedly performed with burial of the dead. Bones are usually found in articulated position, indicating that burial occurred soon after death. The body may have been wrapped in a blanket or woven mat although such perishable materials have not survived. Offerings of ceramic vessels placed with the corpse most likely contained

Village stage figurines show a spontaneity not repeated in later periods. This Oaxaca Valley, San Jose phase personage wears a necklace and monkey (?) mask, probably ritual attire.

26

od and drink to accompany the deceased on the journey to the xt world.

Burial treatment varied. Often an elongated grave was prepared to ceive a body in extended position although some were interred on eir sides in flexed position; others appear to have been stuffed unremoniously into an abandoned pit, suggesting that these individuals ere of little importance to the living.

OLUTION OF THE VILLAGE STAGE

This stage was a time of change as we can see by looking at highhts from the three successive periods within it. During the first two riods, the Red-on-Buff horizon and the Olmec horizon , sites in axaca show clear connections with other areas of Mesoamerica. (The rm "horizon," as used by archaeologists, refers to the presence of me similar cultural elements over a wide geographic area during a latively short time.) In contrast, local development, varying from gion to region, is the most striking aspect of the final period of the illage stage.

he Red-on-Buff horizon: 1500 - 1200 B.C.

This period is named for its characteristic brown to buff pottery with d slip or painted decoration. Simple hemispherical bowls and globular rs with tall necks are the principal vessel forms. This pottery occurs the highlands from Oaxaca to the Basin of Mexico, that is, in the tomangue area previously mentioned. The coastal tradition flourished the Isthmus at this time and is represented in Oaxaca by the site Laguna Zope near Juchitán.

Villages became well established; this was the first period of major pulation expansion. As populations grew, communities fissioned d new villages were founded in the same region. Innovations in social d political organization which might have led to growth within comunities, apparently did not occur.

A population estimate can be obtained based on archaeological cavation. Houses are small and tend to have only a few associated rials, so we estimate average household size at five members. By mple-excavating an entire village we can determine how many houseolds were present; early villages had from three to 10 households. the Valley of Oaxaca, for example, about 30 sites have been located r this period. If there were 25 people per village, the population ould have been roughly 750. Villages were established in all corners the valley from Huitzo in the northwest to Mitla in the east and nearly Ejutla in the south. However, the main concentration was around San sé Mogote in the Etla Valley.

Villages within and between regions were linked by exchanges. or example, obsidian from sources in Veracruz, Puebla, and central lexico was brought into highland Oaxaca, and highland villages obined marine shell and freshwater shell from the Gulf and Pacific

coasts. Pottery figurines, red hematite (naturally occurring iron or
pigment used for pottery making and in rituals, and probably ma
perishable goods — feathers, wooden masks, headdresses — were al
exchanged. All villages seem to have participated in the exchan
network. This contact functioned to transmit not only goods but al
techniques, for example, of pottery making and agriculture, as well
ideas and beliefs.

The complementary trends of unity and diversity are evident duri
the Red-on-Buff horizon . At one level, groups throughout Mesoameri
were in contact through trade. At the same time, on another level, loc
linguistic and cultural patterns were being formed.

The Olmec horizon : 1200 - 850 B.C.

The second main division of the Village stage corresponds chrono
logically to the initial flourishing on the Gulf Coast of Veracruz of th
Olmec culture, which is especially well known for the huge sculpture
basalt heads thought to be portraits of Olmec leaders.

Most relevant for Oaxaca is the appearance at this time of a grou
of pan-Mesoamerican symbols, related and standardized designs tha
had cultural significance as well as decorative function. "Pan-Mes
american" indicates that these designs occur widely throughout Mes
america. The symbols are found most commonly on pottery, but the
also occur on stone artifacts and monuments. They perhaps are evide
most frequently in the Olmec area proper, but no one has determine
with certainty where they originated. The appearance of these symbo
is the beginning of written expression, a key feature of Mesoamerica
civilization.

Why do these symbols occur over such a wide area? and what
they mean? Many of the symbols represent animals that have unusu
power, strength, ferocity — and may present danger to humans: ja
uars, serpents, crocodiles (caiman), and eagles. As animals possesse
of power, they have extrahuman powers. They represent the natur
world, which is separate from the human. They may have been thoug
of as having control over this extrahuman, natural world.

Symbolization has several meanings and implications. First,
symbolize something is to control it. By representing these animals
symbols, villagers were exercising control over them; the villagers ha
"domesticated" the threats present in their natural environment. Th
in a sense the human species had separated itself from its environme
and the natural world.

Second, to represent the animals was also to take control of th
extrahuman forces they embodied. A clear example is the Olmec re
resentation of so-called werejaguars, combinations of man and jagu
Animals are fused with humans, as are their powers. We know fro
later times that there is another class of powerful, natural phenome
of great importance to Mesoamerican groups — rain, lightning, eart
quakes, sun, wind — which we consider inanimate. These phenomen

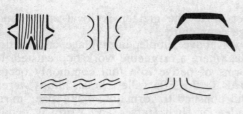
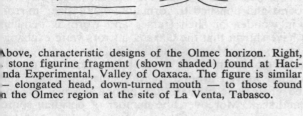
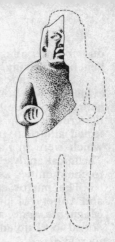

Above, characteristic designs of the Olmec horizon. Right, a stone figurine fragment (shown shaded) found at Hacienda Experimental, Valley of Oaxaca. The figure is similar — elongated head, down-turned mouth — to those found in the Olmec region at the site of La Venta, Tabasco.

too, may have been considered animate and embodied by the powerful animals mentioned above. They may have been represented by other symbols as well.

Third, the use of symbols codifies and standardizes meaning. It is possible, in fact highly likely, that common attitudes and beliefs about the natural and supranatural world existed before 1200 B.C. Symbols express these ideas and beliefs, crystallizing them and giving them outward manifestation to be seen, understood, and manipulated.

The question of why a set of symbols was so widespread is perhaps not too difficult to answer. Trade networks established during the Red-on-Buff horizon linked villages all over Mesoamerica and provided ready-made pathways for the dissemination of ideas — and their attendant symbols — among groups belonging to different language families. Yet we can wonder why the same symbols were so popular among various groups. Perhaps the answer is a common desire to control powerful external forces and a need to externalize and formalize beliefs. A symbol appearing in one area would quickly be adopted in others.

In the Valley of Oaxaca, ceramic vessels with symbolic designs have been found with male burials. Males may have had special roles in ritual activities, but this remains to be clarified.

In sum, symbols in this period added a new dimension to village life — the public expression of beliefs. Further, the spread of this innovation among different groups provided a foundation for a common Mesoamerican religion.

Two other significant changes took place in village life in Oaxaca during the Olmec horizon: a change in settlement pattern, and the beginnings of specialization. In the Cañada, the Mixteca Alta, and the Valley of Oaxaca, several small villages were abandoned while relatively large central villages emerged. Whether there was actually overall population decline or simply emigration to larger villages is unclear, as are the reasons behind this change. Centralization may have been

due to intervillage conflict or to the greater political and econom
benefits of living in a large community.

Specialization at a level above simple, intravillage cooperation
evident at San José Mogote, where a magnetite workshop existed. Ma
netite and ilmenite are forms of native iron that commonly occur (
the ground or in stream beds in the Etla valley. Small lumps were co
lected and then ground and polished to form thumbnail size "mirror
which were inlaid in wooden or shell frames and worn as pendan
Technical analyses have shown that the Oaxaca mirrors were exchang
to communities as far away as Morelos and the Gulf Coast of Veracru

The mirror exchange was part of a general increase in quanti
and variety of products moved around in Mesoamerica at this tim
Magnetite, jade, and greenstone objects were among the new produc
added to obsidian and shell. Moreover, the number of obsidian sourc
increased.

Regionalization: 850 - 500 B.C.

During the third and final division of the Village stage, some are
of major population concentration, such as the Valley of Oaxac
emerged as culturally distinct and presumably politically autonomo
regions. The following are some examples, with pottery styles bei
the most distinctive indicator.

The Valley of Oaxaca. During the Guadalupe (850 - 700 B.C.) and Rosar
(700 - 500 B.C.) phases (two distinctive Valley of Oaxaca periods named f
sites in the region), gray ware became the dominant pottery for serving vesse
initiating the long tradition of Oaxaca gray ware that continues today in what
called the "black pottery" of San Bartolo Coyotepec. There was less empha
on incised designs and symbols on the pottery than in the previous, Olmec horizo
although one design, the St. Andrew's Cross, or "pennant motif," is commo
Little frog heads modeled on bowl rims occur in Late Rosario times, and t
first *comales* or tortilla griddles appear, signaling the "invention" of the tortill
Many ceramic characteristics lead directly into those of the subsequent Ear
Monte Albán I period.

The Valley of Oaxaca encompassed about 80 communities and an estimat
population of 2,000 during the Rosario phase. Now we find clear indicatio
of status differences at both the community and household levels.

Most settlements were hamlets or villages with about 25 inhabitants a
covering some two hectares (five acres). However, one community, San Jo
Mogote had around 500 inhabitants and covered about 40 hectares (100 acres
It had unique status, being centrally located within the Etla Valley and presur
ably having some kind of economic, political, and ceremonial control over near
villages. The construction of large civic-ceremonial buildings may have be
initiated at San José Mogote, reflecting its special role.

Status difference at the household level is evident at the large site of Barr
del Rosario in the town of Huitzo. Two kinds of houses were present: the simp
wattle-and-daub houses commonly found in the Village stage and a much larg
house built atop a white-plastered, one-meter high adobe platform reached l
a staircase. The larger house was probably occupied by an elite family and t
simple houses by common folk.

More excavation is needed to determine how elite families functioned with

30

community at this time, and exactly what San José Mogote's dominant role was. Whatever their precise nature, these status differences indicate formation of a culturally distinct local polity within the Valley of Oaxaca, foreshadowing the emergence of the urban center of Monte Albán.

The Nochixtlán Valley. Etlatongo was the main community here. Distinctive pottery in this valley includes thin, reddish black bowls and red-slipped bowls with white-slipped, incised rim bands.

At Apoala, on the eastern edge of the Mixteca Alta, there is Valley of Oaxaca style, Rosario phase pottery, which perhaps indicates a Zapotec-Mixtec border in this area.

Mixteca Baja. Thin brown pottery found at the site of Santa Teresa near Huajuapan may link this valley with the Nochixtlán Valley and/or with the Puebla-Cholula area to the northwest.

Cañada. Ceramics from Hacienda Tecomaxtlahua could be stylistically related to Tehuacán Valley ceramics.

Southern Isthmus. The coastal tecomate tradition continued. The largest site known in the region for this period is Laguna Zope near Juchitán, which covered about 90 hectares (225 acres); it was important as a center of shell ornament production and as a major link in the trade network connecting the Isthmus to other regions.

Nejapa Valley. A small site in this as yet unstudied region has yielded white-slipped tecomates, suggesting possible links with the Isthmus coastal tradition.

Chinantla. An occupation of this period at Ayotzintepec is probably related to Gulf Coast groups.

Regionalization in the period 850 - 500 B.C. was counterbalanced, just as in previous periods, by interregional trade networks. Obsidian was a major commodity. Jade and greenstone now became highly sought after, widely popular materials. White-slipped pottery was common all over Mesoamerica at this time; much of it was locally produced, demonstrating that techniques as well as materials were transmitted across regions.

By the end of the Village stage, the Valley of Oaxaca had advanced considerably in population and cultural differentiation, preparing the way for the next major step, the emergence of cities and a complex society.

Right, the pennant motif appeared frequently incised on bowls in the Rosario phase. Frog effigy bowls, left, were also common. Fish and duck effigies were fashioned in period Monte Albán I.

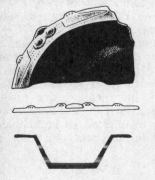
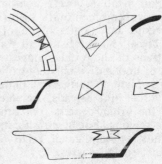

THE URBAN STAGE — TOWNS AND CITIES:
500 B.C. - A.D. 750

The emergence of the first cities between 500 B.C. and 200 B.C marked another major transformation in ancient Oaxaca. Monte Albár was the first urban center in Oaxaca and eventually became the largest Yucuita, Huamelulpan, Diquiyú, Cerro de las Minas, and others formec in the Mixteca, and by approximately A.D. 300 urban centers were present in nearly all regions of Oaxaca. Thus far, however, only the Valley of Oaxaca and the Mixteca centers have been well documentec through archaeological excavations.

Early pre-Hispanic "cities" in Oaxaca had a special character Although they were pre-industrial, agricultural communities, thei size and monumental architecture — buildings constructed on top o huge stone platforms — set them apart from other contemporary set tlements. While they cannot be compared in magnitude to such 20th century metropoli as Mexico City, Paris or London, they had analogou functions, as centers of political, economic, and religious power.

Like early cities elsewhere in the ancient world, they represented the beginnings of urban life and the first time that large groups of people many of them without kinship ties, lived in the same community Oaxaca's pre-Hispanic urban centers exhibit several characteristic directly observable in the archaeological record that clearly distinguisl the Urban stage from the previous Village stage and indicate a new level of social complexity. One of these, of course, is population size While Village communities usually had no more than 200 inhabitants Monte Albán and other early urban centers grew to 2,000 or more shortly after their founding.

A second Urban stage characteristic is monumental architecture Stone and adobe platforms, temples, palaces, and other large structure were present at all the urban centers.

The development of writing is a third feature. Glyphs—carved o painted symbols—were combined with representations of people anc places to commemorate historical events and ritual celebrations, anc to record genealogies of important individuals.

These characteristics all reflect social stratification. The egalitariar relations of the Village stage were no longer dominant; instead certair groups and individuals controlled other people and their labor. This i also evident in settlement patterns which consisted of several levels— individual homesteads, hamlets or villages, intermediate size towns and the urban centers that functioned as political capitals, dominatinᶃ their regions. Social stratification was also manifested in households initially as families of relatively higher or lower status and later a: distinct social classes.

The Great Plaza of Monte Albán is seen here from the air. The access road is to the right of the North Platform, visible at the top of the picture. Among the many structures lining the plaza are: the ball court, upper right; Building J, shaped like an arrowhead, in the southern portion, and the Danzantes building to the left of Building J. The South Platform, facing the North Platform across the immense plaza is largely unexcavated.

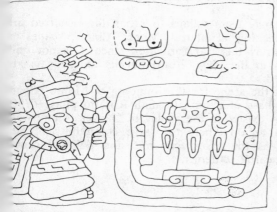

In a wall of Mound III on the South Platform, the stone shown to the left was discovered in 1988. The seated person with an elaborate headdress holds a leaf, suggestive of a hallucinogenic d a t u r a plant, wrapped as an offering b u n d l e. The large framed glyph may indicate a place; above it are partially eroded undeciphered glyphs.

Monte Albán and other urban sites were not simply "ceremonial centers" but cities with extensive residential areas and monumental structures used for various functions. They served as political capitals as well as market and religious centers within their respective regions. Most urban centers, including those on hilltops such as Monte Albán, were located within walking distance of wide expanses of first-class agricultural land where food was grown to support the local population. Thus the agricultural character of Mesoamerican society continued and many urban dwellers were at least part-time farmers.

Descriptions and maps of Oaxaca's best known urban centers, including those frequently visited by tourists, are presented in Site Descriptions at the back of this book. The reader may find it helpful to consult that information while reading this and the following chapter.

The Urban stage in Oaxaca has two main divisions: the Early Urban stage from approximately 500 B.C. to A.D. 250, and the Late Urban stage, from about A.D. 250 to A.D. 750. Although some major differences in the nature of urban society are documented in these two divisions, here the Urban stage will generally be treated as a single period.

The Valley of Oaxaca

Among Valley of Oaxaca sites, Monte Albán was uniquely large in extent and population. (It eventually covered about 6.5 square kilometers and had a population of some 25,000 inhabitants.) Its central location implied a special dominant role within the valley. At the same time, large communities such as Dainzú, Cerro de la Campana (Huijazoo), Lambityeco, and others flourished in the separate branches of the Valley of Oaxaca and evidently functioned as second-level centers. These sites may have had from 500 to 3,000 inhabitants. Monte Albán was a city, so these might best be called towns, although in size they were equivalent to the urban centers or cities of the Mixteca region. Also in the Valley of Oaxaca, both Mitla and Yagul had sizeable Period IIIb-IV occupations and may have functioned as second or third-level centers.

How and why the change from village to urban life occurred are questions of general archaeological interest. Monte Albán provides an unusual opportunity to study this transformation since it is not only one of the earliest cities in the New World but its antecedents are relatively well documented.

Several conditions set the scene for the founding of Monte Albán. First of all, a population base of about 50 small Rosario phase (750–500 B.C.) villages already existed in the Valley of Oaxaca. Many were concentrated in the Etla region where the large community of San José Mogote functioned as the main economic and political center with some control over nearby settlements.

URBAN STAGE
SITES

1. Tequixtepec, 2. Cerro de las Minas, 3. Diquiyú, 4. Huamelulpan, 5. Eloxochi-
lán, 6. Huautla, 7. Quiotepec, 8. Tepeusila, 9. Yucuñudahui, 10. Yucuita, 11. Monte Negro, 12. Cerro de la Campana (Huijazoo), 13. Yucuiní, 14. Monte Albán,
15. Ixtepeji, 16. Dainzú, 17. Lambityeco, 18. Jalieza, 19. San Juan Luvina,
20. Atepec, 21. Ayotzintepec, 22. Río Manzo, 23. Juquila Mixes, 24. La Ladrillera, 25. El Guexe, 26. Nopala, 27. Río Grande, 28. Río Viejo.

Second, certain locations in the Monte Albán area were particularly
favorable with respect to such resources as clay suitable for pottery,
chert for stone tools, salt, and limestone used in preparing corn. This
allowed some villagers to practice specialization in addition to their
normal crop cultivation. In other words, there was differential distribution of some basic resources and possible conflict over who had
access to and control over them.

Third, in the center of the valley the uninhabited island of hills
that later became Monte Albán offered firewood, space for house
construction, land for rainy-season cultivation, and springs with water
for domestic use. All of this made it an attractive place for settlement.
Later, as the city grew, supplies of wood and water were depleted
and the fertility of the hill slopes declined leading to changes in the
organization of the city.)

Around 500 B.C., one or several small communities were founded
on the slopes of Monte Albán. The initial settlers evidently came from
villages in the Valley of Oaxaca since there is continuity between the
Rosario phase and Period I in such things as household organization,
burial treatment, and pottery styles. However, we do not know from
which village(s) they came or what mechanisms provoked their move.
Two possibilities seem likely. One is that they were people from San
José Mogote who left because of internal conflict. A second is that
they were villagers from Tierras Largas, Xoxocotlán, and other communities around the base of Monte Albán who may have been in
conflict with villagers from San José Mogote and Etla Valley.

35

Once present at Monte Albán, these families became the focus of a new organization. Because of its central location, Monte Albán was the logical place to establish a market and coordinate other inter community activities. Specialized products—pottery, chert, salt, lime and others—were brought to Monte Albán and made available through the market to other communities. Once the market was established Monte Albán's growth was exponential. Many people probably emigrated to Monte Albán from villages in the valley. By 100 B.C. the population had grown to about 10,000 inhabitants, and new forms of social and political organization and ceremonial integration emerged

Other, unique aspects of Monte Albán's location also came into play. The main hilltop, commanding a view of nearby branch valleys can be seen from afar and is naturally defensible. In addition, Monte Albán is surrounded by prime alluvial land that can provide two crops per year; calculations show that about 17,500 people could have been supported by production within an eight-kilometer radius of the Main Plaza during Period I. Outcrops of sedimentary rock, rare or absent in many parts of the valley, provided readily available material for house foundations, monumental buildings, and carved stones.

Thus we hypothesize that urban life at Monte Albán began with concentration and redistribution of resources, probably stimulated initially by competition between local groups. Within a few centuries Monte Albán became the dominant, central community in the Valley of Oaxaca, just as San José Mogote had been the principal one in the Etla Valley during the Village stage.

From the time of its founding Monte Albán would have affected other communities with which it had contact and may have led to the formation of urban centers in nearby regions. The origin of these centers, though, is less well understood because their pre-urban ante cedents are poorly documented.

The Mixteca Alta and Baja

Many small urban centers emerged in the valleys of the rugged mountainous Mixteca region. These centers had from 500 to 3,000 inhabitants, depending on the extent of the surrounding valley and the amount of cultivable land nearby. In contrast to the Valley of Oaxaca where Monte Albán was unique in size, influence, and power no single center dominated in the Mixteca. Nevertheless, the Mixteca urban centers reflect several interesting and significant patterns. For example, many of them are separated by roughly a day's walk. A person carrying a load can walk about 30 kilometers on uneven terrain in a day (eight to 12 hours). The following sites are separated by approximately that distance: Cerro de las Minas and Diquiyú; Cerro de las Minas and Yatachio; Tejupan and Cerro Jazmín; Yucuita and Monte Negro; Monte Negro and Huamelulpan. Within the Nochixtlán Valley the largest of the valleys in the Mixteca, sites such as Cerro Jazmín Yucuita, and Etlatongo are closer to each other than 30 km. and i

Left, Yucuiní, a naturally defensible ridge top site in the Mixteca Alta just west of the Etla Valley. The present-day village of San Mateo Tepantepec is on the slope to the right of the ridge. Above, a Ramos phase ceramic head with mask from Yucuita may represent a warrior.

may be that at any given time only one of them was a principal center.

Distances between sites probably played a role in the formation of local polities. A local urban center could effectively control and dominate populations within a radius of about half a day's walk, or 15 km. (hence perhaps the 30 km. or so distance between centers). This distance would be practical for marketing and festivities: in one day people could walk to the center, participate in some activity, and return home; or people from the center could travel to dependent communities, carry out some administrative task, and return.

There are several indications of conflict in Early Urban times. Early Urban centers tended to be located on hilltops. Cerro de las Minas, Diquiyú, and Monte Negro, for example, are on points which visually dominate the surroundings and from which attackers could be driven back from above. Stone constructions added to their defensive character in nearly every case. At Yucuita a huge stone wall along the east side of the site would have prevented access to the site center except through controllable stairways and tunnels. One tunnel-passageway has a sharp prow-shaped stone placed at a low level so that anyone unfamiliar with the tunnel might have split his skull open in trying to run through it.

Trophy skulls are another possible indicator of Early Urban stage conflict. Whole examples and fragments have been found at Huameulpan, Yucuita, and Monte Negro. Two small holes drilled in the top of the skull after death were used to suspend the skull with a cord, perhaps from a roof beam or possibly as a pendent on a necklace.

Occupations at some Early Urban centers may have been interrupted. Yucuita was apparently abandoned around the time of Christ, possibly because of conflicts. Construction ceased on some major buildings and others may have been burned; refugees from Yucuita may have fled to Monte Negro. Monumental construction at Cerro de las Minas is principally of Early Urban date, and there seems to have been a hiatus in its occupation before Late Urban stage buildings were constructed.

Weapons could provide archaeological clues to conflict, but clearly identifiable weapons are rarely found. Later, in City-State times, obsidian blades were inlaid along the edge of a broad wooden sword, and this weapon may have been present much earlier. Blades are found commonly at Urban stage sites but those used as weapons have not been distinguished from those used domestically.

The spear-thrower and bow and arrow were known and used in Oaxaca as early as the Lithic stage and, along with clubs, could have served equally well as weapons or as hunting implements. Chipped-stone arrow points have been found in Late Urban context with male burials at Yucuita.

In general, the Mixteca centers appear to have been competing polities, in contact with one another but often involving hostility and raiding. Geographic separation would suggest that competition was not for land or goods, but rather between leaders for power and prestige. Yet a number of elements show that the Mixteca centers were linked. Some examples are similar projectile-point styles, similar architectural techniques involving cellular construction (rectangles formed by retaining walls filled with rock and dirt rubble) in the enlargement of platforms, presence of lipped metates in Early Urban times, trophy skulls, and the use of a dagger-like motif on carved stones and other representations. However, the hilltop placements, a clear departure from Village-stage settlement locations, indicate that interactions were often less than friendly.

An interesting question is what linguistic and ethnic group or groups were associated with urban centers in the Mixteca. The most parsimonius and simplest interpretation is that they were Mixtec speakers. As mentioned in the previous chapter, it seems likely that the people who established Village stage occupations in the Mixteca belonged to the Mixtecan branch of the Otomangue language family. In Early Urban times there was a great population increase and people moved out from areas of Village stage settlement, such as the Nochixtlán Valley, to set up new communities. Groups within the Mixteca apparently had common roots and remained in contact. Yet the Mixteca urban centers were clearly different from the Valley of Oaxaca (Zapotec) settlements of the same period in terms of pottery, some architectural elements, details of burial customs, and so forth.

Thus while we know little about total variation within the Mixteca in Early Urban times, there are cultural patterns indicating some unity within the region and differentiation from other areas.

Urban stage social organization grew out of Village stage ante-edents. This is reflected most clearly at the household level, while tratification and tribute are significant new aspects of Urban stage ociety.

Households

The nuclear or small extended-family household continued as the asic social unit during the Urban stage. In Early Urban times most ouseholds produced, stored, and consumed their own food and buried heir dead near or beneath the floors of the residence. However, some atterns of daily life changed, compared to the Village stage, and ivision of labor became more complex. In Early Urban times greater uantities of nonlocal goods became available to households, suggest-ig increased trade and production of special goods. For example, the mount of imported obsidian used for domestic tasks increased in Early Jrban times over what was available in the Village stage. The variety f pottery vessel forms also increased in Early Urban times, indicating nore diversity in foods and their preparation.

Two vessel forms are particularly notable—the *comal* and the uchilquitongo bowl. The comal, or tortilla griddle, appeared initially t the end of the Village stage; in Early Urban times it became common nd was found in all households in the highlands, at least in the Mixteca nd the Valley of Oaxaca. Presence of the comal implies preparation f tortillas, still the most common form of corn consumption today. Corn is soaked overnight in water with lime. The kernels swell and often, making them easier to grind, hull and all, on the metate. The prepared dough, called *masa* in Spanish, is patted into thin discs, then aked lightly on the comal which resembles a round cookie sheet made f pottery. Tortillas, like masa, are moist and get moldy after a day or so. But they can be made into *tostadas* by placing them on the uter edge of the hot comal, where they become crisp and completely lried out. Tostadas can be conserved for weeks. They can be carried y workers who go from a village to the city to work for several days, y itinerant merchants, or by farmers who stay out in their fields work-ng for a few days during planting or harvesting season.

The Suchilquitongo bowl is a pottery mortar, a circular bowl with hree solid feet, thick walls, and usually evidence of wear on the in-erior from grinding. These bowls, of cream paste ("paste" is the echnical term for prepared clay) were produced in the Atzompa-Cacao-epec area just northwest of Monte Albán. (The name derives from ome complete examples found near the town of Suchilquitongo at the

Staples of the Mexican
liet — tortillas and
sauces — had their
origins more than 2,000
year ago with the comal
and the Suchilquitongo
bowl.

39

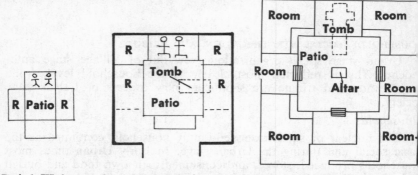

Period III houses from Monte Albán. The simplest apparently had cane and mud walls; intermediate-size houses, built of adobe set on stone foundations, had simple graves as well as tombs. The "palaces" were built on a grander scale.

northwest end of the Etla Valley.) They were apparently used for preparing sauces or condiments, probably of chile, tomato, or other plants. Sauces evidently became popular immediately over a wide area since Suchilquitongo bowls are found throughout the Valley of Oaxaca and occasionally at sites in the Mixteca Alta, the Cañada, and as far away as the Tehuacán Valley in Puebla.

Social Stratification

Egalitarian relations prevailed during the Village stage even though some status differentiation was evident between households. In Early Urban times, however, social stratification was marked and relations of inequality predominated. E rly Urban sites have revealed both relatively higher and lower status households. Low-status households were similar to those of the Village stage, that is, they were nuclear families. Archaeologically, they are represented by individual family dwellings of open or semi-closed format with storage pits, ovens, burials, and work areas in the adjacent yard or patio. Space between households was used for kitchen gardens or small corn fields.

High-status households, on the other hand, had more members; they were probably extended families plus their dependents and servants. Houses were large with more rooms and relatively elaborate construction such as thick walls and stucco floors. Some residences had a closed format, that is, their rooms surrounded a square central patio. Some had large storage rooms or unusually large bell-shaped storage pits. One pit at Yucuita for example, measured 12 cubic meters, and a residence excavated at Huamelulpan had a cache of large serving vessels, perhaps used by the family for providing food during community festivities.

Burial treatment also reflected social status of households. Whereas commoners were usually buried in simple graves with perhaps one or two vessels, elite individuals were sometimes interred in formal tombs constructed of stone and with offerings of dozens of ceramic vessels along with such luxury items as jade earspools and stone bead necklaces.

The status distinction between households suggests that elite families controlled some of the labor and/or labor product of commoners. Interestingly, there were elite families even in the smaller Early Urban communities. A family in each village was apparently responsible for controlling production and labor within the village and was linked through alliances, kinship, or both, to elite leaders at the urban center.

The urban centers themselves were divided into neighborhoods, each with at least one leading family and numerous low-status families. In other words, in Early Urban times there was a social group intermediate between the individual household and the community: the group of interdependent households comprising an elite-administrative family and its dependents. There is no evidence indicating presence of a supreme leader or ruler; leadership may have been based on a council of elders composed of representatives from elite families in different villages and/or neighborhoods.

Tribute and Classes in Late Urban Times

Early Urban society in Oaxaca was flexible, dynamic, and open. As urban populations grew, they exerted pressure on local resources such as land, water, firewood, building materials, and wild plants and animals. This led to increased competition, and formalization and regularization of use and ownership of resources. It also resulted in the implementation of a tribute system in which dependent communities were required to contribute goods and services to the urban centers. In exchange they received protection and the right to participate in the markets and ceremonies at the urban centers. Refusal to participate or to provide tribute presumably led to conflict and the use of force. The ultimate effect of urban growth was thus the transformation of a flexible society into a formalized, relatively rigid society of distinct social classes. This process took place in Oaxaca between 100 B.C. and A.D. 300, and by Late Urban times the change was established.

During Late Urban times in the Valley of Oaxaca and the Mixteca (and probably elsewhere), there were at least three social classes reflected in three types of households. At Monte Albán, for example, these are manifested archaeologically by three kinds of residences. All three exhibit a standard format, consisting of rooms arranged around a closed central patio with burials and tombs below a room or the patio floor. The simplest, smallest houses had thin walls, possibly of cane or brush; family members were buried in slab-lined graves beneath room floors. Intermediate size houses had thick adobe walls and a tomb beneath the patio as well as simple, slab-lined graves. Large houses or palaces had thick stone wall foundations, steps leading from the patio up to the rooms, and sub-patio tombs sometimes painted with murals such as those in Tombs 103, 104, and 105 at Monte Albán. The large, elegant Tomb 5 at Cerro de la Campana (Huijazoo) appears to be associated with a palace even larger than those identified at Monte Albán, though this remains to be confirmed through excavation.

41

Commoners may not have stored their own corn and may have had only limited access to products such as obsidian, jade, and ceramic urns. Intermediate status households (possibly administrators and craftsmen) and the large, complex households of elite leaders probably controlled land and the distribution of goods. In Late Urban times the elite also controlled most of the fine artistic work such as painted murals, urns, carved bone, carved stones, and jewelry, all found primarily in large tombs.

ARCHITECTURE AT URBAN CENTERS

Monumental architecture added a new dimension to life during the Urban stage. As local political capitals, urban centers served their own populations as well as dependent communities, and this was done partly through monumental architecture, that is, the creation of centralized communal space and public works. Construction involved cooperation by individuals and groups supervised by specialists.

Architectural Layout of Urban Centers

The layout of urban centers in Oaxaca varies. In general, large, non-residential buildings are found in a central area of the site and residences are distributed around the periphery. At hilltop sites (Monte Albán, Monte Negro, Yucuita, and others), main buildings are found on high points, along high ridges, and on artificially flattened areas while residences are on terraces downslope.

Two kinds of overall architectural layouts are found at the Urban centers. One consists of sites with a central plaza that forms a clear focal point of the city. Monte Albán is the best example, and others are Cerro de las Minas in the Mixteca Baja and Río Viejo on the Coast. During the Urban stage, the town of San José Mogote had a central plaza modeled on that of Monte Albán.

A second, more common layout is that of a generalized central area formed by a conglomeration of buildings with no obvious central plaza. Large buildings were clearly the heart of these cities but the layout was less formal. These cities seem to have grown by accretion with buildings and open spaces strung out along ridges and saddles. At these sites it has not been possible to tell what area, if any, was the focal point. In the future, careful mapping and excavation may reveal more architectural planning than is evident at present.

Building Materials and Construction Techniques

Stone was the preferred construction material for large Urban stage buildings. Some sites, like Monte Albán, Yucuita, and Diquiyú, are situated where naturally occurring limestone and sandstone blocks are readily available. Blocks were quarried and, if necessary, faced and cut to size with stone tools, then placed as the outer walls and stairways of buildings. Irregular chunks of rock served as rubble fill in these buildings.

Some large structures, especially platforms that were essentially bases on top of which houses and temples were constructed, had walls up to seven meters high. Foundation stones were usually placed directly on the ground or just below topsoil level. Had foundations been set in trenches dug into the bedrock, the walls might have been sturdier. Large platforms were occasionally remodeled and rebuilt for the purpose of enlarging the base upon which other structures were raised. If a wall or corner was damaged by an earthquake, for example, removal of stones and rubble from the affected area might have provoked additional collapse, so the best alternative for repair was to enlarge the structure and cover the damaged portion.

Rectangular adobes (sun-dried mud bricks) were usually employed for the walls of houses, temples, and other structures. Adobe walls had foundations made of stone placed exactly the width of the adobes and varying from one to several rows of stones in height.

Stones or adobes were joined with mud mortar to 'form walls. Floors were made of stucco, that is, crushed white lime usually mixed with sand or pea gravel. Both stone and adobe walls were coated with a thin layer of white stucco plaster, so the stone walls visible today at Monte Albán, for example, would have appeared smooth and white while the city was functioning. Roofs were constructed of wooden beams, poles, and thatch, sometimes incorporating a layer of dirt.

Visitors often ask if archaeological sites were deliberately buried. Modification and rebuilding were common and the external dimensions of structures were often enlarged by filling rooms with dirt and rock rubble and constructing new exterior walls. But sites were not intentionally covered with dirt when abandoned. Just as today in Oaxaca, if buildings are not kept up they begin to disintegrate from the action of sun, rain, wind, insects, temperature changes, and earthquakes. Roofs collapse and adobes melt, forming piles of dirt covering the latest floor and wall foundations, and creating mounds like those frequently seen at unexplored archaeological sites.

Retaining Walls

Large stone retaining walls built against hillslopes are common Urban stage structures. Early Urban examples in the Mixteca Alta often have corners of refrigerator-size monoliths. At Yucuita and Diquiyú such walls demarcated the community centers, which were flat areas used for market and ceremonial activities and for construction of other large buildings. These walls also had a defensive function since the site center could be reached only by a limited number of stairways and passages spaced along the huge walls.

Free-Standing Platforms

Platforms, usually with four sides and built in open spaces, were constructed from Early Urban times on. Examples from Monte Albán are the Danzantes Wall, Building J, and Building IV-Sub. All have

Building J, the arrowhead-shaped structure at Monte Albán, has remnants of temple on top but its unusual shape has yet to be explained.

walls formed by huge monoliths that must have been moved fror nearby quarries and set up by work groups of many men. These plat forms are not complete structures but rather foundations, probably fo temples. We lack information on the floor plans of the buildings o top of these platforms so their functions remain unknown, although the were probably of a ritual or administrative nature. Except for Buildin J, these platforms lack stairways; they may have had wooden stairways or if stone stairways existed they were removed when the building were remodeled. Free-standing rectangular platforms at Yucuita an Monte Negro have walls over two meters high. They also lack evidenc of stairways and their function is similarly problematical.

Arrowhead-Shaped Buildings

Building J at Monte Albán and Building O at the small site of Ca ballito Blanco near Yagul in the Tlacolula Valley are free-standing plat forms shaped like a ship's prow or arrowhead. They are roughly con temporaneous and correspond to Late Period I or Period II. Apparentl because of its peculiar shape and the northwest-southeast passagewa through the point, Alfonso Caso suggested that Building J might hav been an observatory. Since then many people have assumed that i was an observatory, even though no conclusive evidence has been pu forth to support Caso's hypothesis. The passageway is slightly curve and neither doorway appears to be oriented toward significant astro nomical phenomena.

Several other possibilities have been suggested as well. The prov points to a place in the southwest where at about the time of Christ when the building was constructed, several of the brightest stars in th sky would have set in the dawn sky. No significant archaeological site have been found in this direction. A line perpendicular to the stairwa on the northeast side of the building and aligned with the top of Build ing P points to a place on the horizon where Capella, one of th brightest stars, rises at about the time of the sun's zenith passage. I other words, Capella's rising at a specific point on the eastern horizo would have heralded the zenith passage. However, we do not know what was on top of Building P and what structures there may have blocked the view.

None of these suggestions is precise enough to be convincing, so Building J's shape remains a puzzle. The incised stones forming part of its walls suggest the building had a commemorative significance although it is not known how these carved slabs related to the building's unusual shape.

The arrowhead-shaped building at Caballito Blanco points to a different place on the horizon than Building J, and the orientation is similarly unexplained. There may be another arrowhead-shaped building not yet excavated in the plaza at San José Mogote.

Temples

Temples appear as a distinct type of building during Early Urban times. Doorways are wide in contrast to the closed, private entrances of residences. Early temples at Monte Negro and in the Valley of Oaxaca consist of two rooms joined on their long walls, with wide doorways and columns at the front, perhaps to support a roof. This remarkably long-lived architectural format lasted until the Conquest. Temples were usually built atop raised platforms, sometimes inaccurately called "pyramids." By raising the temple, spectators or participants gathered below would have had a view of ceremonies, while priests or officials standing at the temple doorway would have commanded the attention of onlookers.

Temple-Patio-Altar

In Late Urban times a formalized ritual-ceremonial precinct, the temple-patio-altar compound (TPA), was common in the Zapotec area. The TPA consists of a large enclosed patio with a small raised platform or altar in the center and a temple situated atop a platform on one

Temples in the TPA complexes had stone wall foundations, adobe walls, roofs probably made of wooden poles and thatch, and sometimes columns in front of the doorway to support a porch roof.

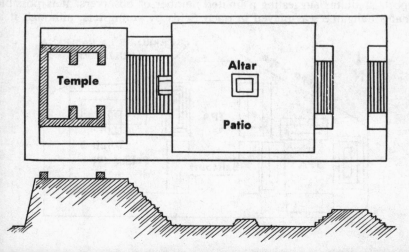

Left, the ballcourt at Dainzú where the game received special emphasis. Below, the ballcourt at Huijazoo is associated with a palace and two TPAs.

side of the patio. Walls or lower platforms usually delimited the other three sides of the patio. The TPA, analogous to a church and atrium today, would have been used for religious rites. Ethnohistoric data suggest that the altar may have been used for making offerings or (presumably animal) sacrifices.

Ballcourts

Pre-Hispanic ballcourts in Oaxaca are shaped like a capital I. The long axis was the playing field and the ball probably was bounced off the sloping side walls. (The tiny stone "steps" now visible in the walls of some ballcourts, such as the one bordering the Main Plaza at Monte Albán, were covered by a thick layer of stucco plaster forming a smooth, inclined surface.) Some ballcourts in Oaxaca have niches in opposite corners of the end areas; whether these were goals or spaces for offerings is not known. The precise rules of the game are also unknown.

Some ballcourts are associated with high-status residences and the TPA architectural unit which may indicate either that the elite played the ballgame or they controlled who played. A good example of this association is present at Cerro de la Campana (Huijazoo) in the Etla Valley where the structures date back to Period IIIb-IV. There is little spectator space around pre-Hispanic ballcourts in contrast to modern sports stadiums suggesting a limited number of observers. It is possible that a ballgame was played in open fields by youngsters, although it is

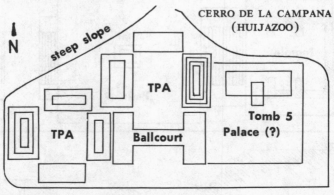

doubtful that everyone had access to imported rubber balls. Thus several lines of evidence suggest that the game was played by elite groups, perhaps associated with ritual or political activities.

The ball (imported from the Gulf Coast lowlands) used in the game was smaller than a baseball, judging from the depictions at Dainzú. The Dainzú stones also show that special protective head and arm gear was worn. The game presumably involved two individuals or teams of several members. The aim apparently was to hit the ball with elbows, hips, feet, or some other part of the body and move it into the opponent's territory. Differences among Mesoamerican ballcourts suggest that there were variations in the game, and rules may have changed from place to place. For example, some Mesoamerican ballcourts, but not those in Oaxaca, have rings in the side walls that may have been goals to hit the ball through.

Today in the Valley of Oaxaca and the Mixteca Alta a game called *pelota mixteca* (Mixtec ball) is played. It is probably a direct descendant of the pre-Hispanic game. A heavy, solid rubber ball about 12 centimeters in diameter is used. The court is long and narrow, and a team of several men stands at each end. Each player wears a heavy leather glove with metal studs forming a hitting surface. The ball is bounced off a stone slab (similar stones have been found in some pre-Hispanic ballcourts) and served by hitting it to the opposing team. The ball travels fast and bounces sharply. It is hit back and forth in the air or on one bounce until it goes outside the court or is missed by one team. Points are scored to determine the winning team.

Water Control Systems

Constructions related to water control are common in the urban centers. During the rainy season, households captured rain water and run-off in their patios for domestic use. Stone-lined drains were used to channel water from large storms out of patios and plazas. Some

The tunnel in this platform at Yucuita served as a water control feature and as a passageway leading up to the site center. A prow-shaped stone placed low in the tunnel would have discouraged the unwanted visitor.

drains are spacious passages that also served as tunnels connecting buildings.

At Monte Albán, a water storage cistern in the Main Plaza was apparently filled by rain run-off. Water that fell in the Sunken Patio and the Main Plaza at Monte Albán was conducted to ravines on the hillsides and from there flowed down to dams at the foot of the hill. On the Xoxocotlán side, the water was then channeled through narrow irrigation canals to cultivated fields. On the northwest side of Monte Albán, water was held in a large reservoir which possibly provided water for domestic use early in the dry season. After a few months this supply would have been exhausted and residents of Monte Albán (and hilltop sites elsewhere in Oaxaca) would have had to walk to springs at the base of the hill, to wells dug in the river bottom alluvium, or to nearby rivers to obtain water for domestic use.

SYMBOLS, HISTORY, AND RELIGION

Symbols became extremely important during the Urban stage. Zapotecs in the Valley of Oaxaca devised a sophisticated and complex set of symbols which, together with the Maya system of notation, is counted among Mesoamerica's earliest writing systems.

Artistic expression flourished in conjunction with the use of symbols. Highly skilled, specialized craftsmen produced such works of art as carved stones, ceramic urns, painted murals, stuccoed sculptures, and engraved bone and stone. They also must have used perishable materials—wood, cloth, leather, and bark paper—though such artifacts are rarely preserved.

Our writing is phonetic and employs symbols (letters) to make words from combinations of sounds. Pre-Hispanic Zapotec writing, however, was not so simple; it was probably partly phonetic (some glyphs represented sounds) and partly ideographic, where certain glyphs stood for ideas. However, we don't know exactly when these different principles were operative. Since the Zapotec language of 2,000 years ago varied significantly from today's Zapotec, we cannot rely directly on present-day linguistics to interpret the glyphs. Furthermore, since some glyphs appeared in various regions and were used during many centuries, their meanings must have varied depending on temporal and ethnic context. So, although studies by Alfonso Caso, and, more recently, by Gordon Whittaker and Javier Urcid, have clarified some aspects of Zapotec writing and the use of symbols in ancient Oaxaca in general, other features still remain to be deciphered and explained.

History and power are predominant themes reflected in Zapotec writing and in symbols used elsewhere in Oaxaca. Symbols and writing allowed people to express their identities and locate themselves in time and space. Thus many glyphs have to do with reckoning time, naming people and places, and expressing power.

What must have been symbols of rank and power are displayed on this Urban stage urn from Tomb 12 at San José Mogote. The lower portion shows a face wearing a mouth mask; the upper portion is an elaborate headdress. It is made of gray pottery and shows traces of red and yellow paint. Gray pottery, common in Oaxaca, is produced by reduction firing: during the last half of the firing process vessels are smothered with a layer of dirt to keep out air. In contrast, yellow, red and brown pottery are produced by letting oxygen reach vessels during firing.

Power can be shown literally by depicting human beings with clothing, adornments, and postures that correspond to high status in real life. Earspools and bead necklaces shown on carved stones, for example, are probably similar to jewelry actually worn by elite personages.

Power can also be shown using costumes such as masks and headdresses in conjunction with symbols that mean the wearer acquires some extrahuman qualities. The wearer of a mask takes on another face and is empowered to speak words of special significance. Headdresses are like crowns: they may indicate rank or, like masks, acquisition of special attributes of another creature. In real life, leaders and priests must have worn masks, headdresses, and other garb as manifestations of their power and authority over other members of society.

Space and Time

To record a historical event means to locate it in space and time. In pre-Hispanic Zapotec writing, place was indicated by a glyph resembling an artificial stepped platform. A symbol naming the place (a toponymic glyph) was often shown within the frame forming the platform. The Urban-stage place glyph represents an architectural feature—perhaps the palace or temple of a ruling family, though it may stand for the entire community. (Later, during the City-State stage, the place glyph was drawn as a rounded, nearly conical hill and looks like a natural feature rather than an artificial one.)

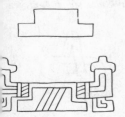

Left above, the Urban stage basic place glyph (stepped platform); below, the adorned place glyph, Building J type, may represent Monte Albán. Right, the City-State place glyph, a hill, bottom, followed by a black and white stepped-fret band, symbol for Tilantongo, topped by a temple, a frequent element in City-State toponyms.

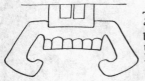

Two examples of the "jaws of the sky" or sky band; on the right is the stylized version. Many variations exist.

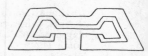

Another convention used for locating people in space is the glyph Alfonso Caso called "jaws of the sky." It frequently appears above human figures on carved stones and painted murals. The place glyph and the sky jaws (or sky band) frame the human figure, locating it symbolically between the earth and the sky.

Seen from the front, the Zapotec "jaws of the sky" symbol appears as a stylized jaguar face with teeth and snarling mouth. However, it is bilaterally symmetrical and each half represents in profile the Wide-Billed Bird, a prominent Zapotec deity. In profile the jaguar's teeth become the bird's eyes; perhaps the deity derives from a mythical bird-jaguar combination. This expression of the sky is a way of making it stand still or at least fixing, controlling, or "domesticating" it. Here again we see the principle, present in the Village stage, of attributing animal (part real, part mythical) characteristics to unknown, powerful forces.

How did people locate things in time? Several natural cycles could have been counted to mark time. The diurnal cycle of day and night is obvious, as is the lunar cycle of approximately 28 days. The longer cycle of Venus may also have been observed and is known to have been recorded by the Maya. The yearly cycle of the sun's movement would have been evident. The question, of course, is whether these natural cycles actually were recorded in ancient Oaxaca and what symbols represented them.

A solar calendar of 365 days must have been used in Oaxaca. The Maya and later Mesoamerican groups employed a solar calendar of 360 days (divided into 20 months of 18 days each) plus five extra days. Some undeciphered Zapotec glyphs may represent solar months.

Alfonso Caso identified one of the common symbols at Monte Albán as a "year sign," that is, a glyph indicating that the temporal unit on an inscription refers to a solar year. The Zapotec year sign is a headdress shown in profile. Similar headdresses are sometimes represented on ceramic braziers and urns that depict men in ceremonial costume. Use of a headdress for the year sign may indicate that certain

Three year glyphs, from left to right: *Urban stage*, Zapotec, headdress in profile; *Late Urban stage*, headdress front view, forerunner of *City-State stage* A-O year sign used in codices.

1 ○ ◐ ◉ **7**

5 ▭ ▱ ⌐ **10**

powerful people understood and perhaps manipulated the calendrical cycles. (In Late Urban times another type of headdress is often shown face-on rather than in profile; it may be the prototype for the A-O year sign used in the City-State stage.)

Reckoning time requires counting, and in Urban stage Oaxaca numerals were expressed in standard Mesoamerican fashion: a dot represented one and a bar represented five. Dots were sometimes embellished with a point or crescent in the center, or were shown as a U. Bars were sometimes decorated with diagonal lines or bands, as if they were sticks used for counting and tied in a bundle; curved bars are occasionally depicted.

A 260-day calendar was used in Oaxaca from Early Urban times, and was later present in most areas of Mesoamerica. It is known as the ritual calendar, *pije* or *piye* in Zapotec. In this calendar time was expressed by a combination of 13 numerals and 20 symbols representing days (20 x 13 = 260). Caso classified the common Zapotec glyphs into groups and designated them Glyph A, Glyph B, Glyph C, and so forth; many are day signs in the ritual calendar. In Oaxaca, as in other Mesoamerican areas, a person was sometimes referred to by his birthdate in the ritual calendar, for example, as 8 Deer, 10 Lizard, 5 House, and so on.

Interestingly, both ritual and solar calendrical reckonings, based on the pre-Hispanic calendars, are still used today among some Mixe, southern Zapotec, and other groups in Oaxaca.

Several other glyphs found in Oaxaca probably refer to units of time. The so-called "year bearers" are four day signs of the ritual calendar which appear with the year sign mentioned above. The year bearer is the name of the solar year; it corresponds to the day sign from the ritual calendar that falls on the first day of the solar year. Because of the way the 260-day ritual calendar meshes with the solar calendar, only four of the 20 day signs function as year bearers. The year bearers in the Zapotec calendar, identified by Javier Urcid, are represented by Caso's Glyphs E, G, N and a variant of M. Seasons,

Urban-stage year glyph with the four year bearers (according to Javier Urcid), from left to right: Glyph E, Glyph G, Glyph M (variant), Glyph N.

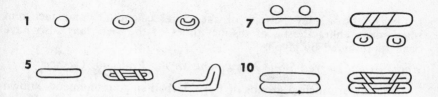

trecenas (the 13-day periods of the ritual calendar), and recurren
phenomena characteristic of distinct times of the year may also have
been represented by glyphs.

Early Urban Carved-Stone Monuments in the Valley of Oaxaca

The three principal groups of Early Urban stage monuments known
in the Valley of Oaxaca are the Danzantes of Monte Albán, the Building J slabs at Monte Albán, and the Ballplayers of Dainzú. Each group
consisted originally of large monoliths placed in platform walls in
prominent positions, suggesting a communal construction effort and
public display of the subject matter carved on the stones. Historical
representations appear to be the theme in each case.

The Danzantes of Monte Albán. The *danzantes* (literally, dancers),
together with the *nadadores* (swimmers), date back to Period I and are
the oldest group of carved stone monuments found thus far in Oaxaca.
Some danzantes are incised, others are carved in low relief on large
monoliths; they depict men in various positions—standing, squatting,
kneeling. The nadadores are human figures in horizontal position carved
or incised on smaller rectangular blocks. Approximately 300 danzantes
and nadadores have been recorded at Monte Albán. Many were originally set in a large wall, the Danzantes Wall, in the southwest corner
of the Main Plaza, then were removed in later periods and incorporated
in other constructions. The preserved portion of the Danzantes Wall
shows alternating rows of danzantes and nadadores built up to a height
of several meters. At the south end of the wall are Stelae 12 and 13,
which show glyphs and dates.

The danzantes appear to be portraits, not abstractions. Some individuals are shown more than once. Some personages have bead necklaces, earspools, and elaborate hairdos. Glyphs in front of their heads
may indicate their names. Several are shown with a glyph resembling
a rattle which, according to Gordon Whittaker, signifies death. Alternatively, the glyph may depict a spear-thrower handle, signifying power.
The large, elaborate danzantes are probably high-status individuals; in
contrast, their smaller size and horizontal position suggest that at least
some of the nadadores represent the general populace. The distinction
between the essentially vertical position of the danzantes and the horizontal orientation of the nadadores may reflect relations of dominance
and submission.

A peculiar aspect of some danzantes is the so-called genital scroll,
on the interior of the thighs or on the abdomen. The wavy lines look
something like the symbol for water or liquid that occurs in other
contexts. The scrolls may represent semen or flowers and symbolize
fertility and/or power. Only in one case is a penis shown, and sometimes instead of a penis there is a circle, which some have taken to
represent genital mutilation.

The Danzantes Wall incorporated all the elements of a history—

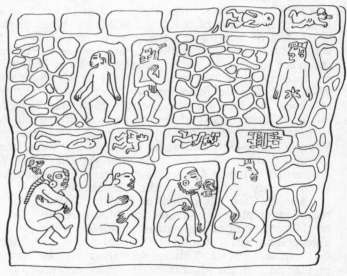

Above, some danzantes are grouped below the wall where they were originally placed. Right, a rendering of a portion of the wall with alternating rows of "dancers" and "swimmers." Note the genital scroll, and the rattle glyphs.

ime, place, actors, and/or events—presented as a narrative analogous to the cloth and animal-skin codices of later times. Stelae 12 and 13, plus other stelae removed from the platform centuries ago, exhibit ime glyphs as well as possible verbs and qualifiers. A hand holding a bar may indicate dominance or subjugation. Place may be indicated on the stelae unless it was understood that Monte Albán itself was the place of reference. The danzantes and nadadores are the actors.

What is the theme of the narrative? The danzantes have been interpreted variously as dancers, slain captives, sick and deformed people, and ecstatic priests. None of the hypotheses is particularly convincing. The individuals appear to be alive; their "strange" positions can be attributed to artistic convention. This was the first time in Oaxaca, or anywhere in Mesoamerica, that an entire gallery of human portraits was produced. To convey a sense of depth and movement on a two-dimensional stone surface, the artists exaggerated, emphasized, and moved certain features—sometimes raising a shoulder, twisting the legs, or bending the arms—to portray what must have been significant postures and gestures. (The ancient Egyptians used analogous artistic techniques, for example, in showing the legs of a striding figure from the side and the torso from the front.) A more likely interpretation is that the wall shows individuals and events related to the founding and early years of Monte Albán. In other words, the wall (and perhaps the entire platform) was a commemorative monument narrating Monte Albán's history. To read it, one would have to reconstruct the order in which the stones were originally placed.

The Building J Slabs at Monte Albán. Approximately 40 large monoliths (sometimes called slabs because of their flat outer surfaces) in the exterior walls of Building J at Monte Albán display incised symbols. Most of them show a repetitive pattern of three elements: in the center is a place glyph, below it is an inverted human head, and above the place glyph is a symbol that varies from slab to slab. In some instances the three central elements are flanked by a text that includes dates and possible references to actors and/or events. The original sequence in which the slabs were placed may have been significant but is unknown; most of the stones were found on the ground, and even in pre-Hispanic times the original order had been scrambled. Since some re-used danzantes occur in the walls, some sections of Building J must have been built after the Danzantes Wall was partly dismantled. Building J is assigned to Period II although it was perhaps contemporary with some of the late danzantes.

Alfonso Caso interpreted the Building J stones as "conquest slabs" representing places conquered by Monte Albán. The inverted head, he claimed, signifies conquest or subjugation; the place glyph provides a geographic referent; and the symbol above each place glyph names that particular place. This interpretation may be correct although, as in the case of the danzantes, it seems doubtful that people would devote so much effort to their enemies. Most societies honor their leaders and heroes, and thus an alternative interpretation is that the Building J slabs commemorate towns that played important roles as allies rather than as enemies in the early history of Monte Albán. The inverted heads may represent individuals, perhaps important local leaders, or they may stand for all the people in a given town. The symbols may indicate names of the towns. As Whittaker has noted, since the place glyph is the same on each slab, it may stand for Monte Albán itself. However, this may simply be an early version of the place glyph

Most Building J slabs have the same three elements: place glyph in the center; above it a symbol that varies from slab to slab, and at the bottom an inverted human head.

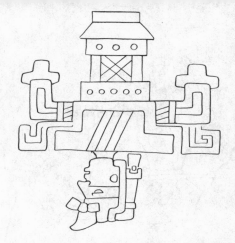

with the place name shown above it rather than incorporated within it as occurs in later examples.

The Building J slabs, like the danzantes, adorn a structure that was visible to all. While the danzantes emphasize people, the Building J slabs emphasize place. The place glyph occupies the central position and the human aspect is de-emphasized since only heads and not entire bodies are shown. However, an interesting similarity is that both the Danzantes Wall and Building J incorporate multiple representations, that is, there are numerous carvings and they show many different people (danzantes) or communities (Building J Slabs). In contrast, most carved stones of later periods are either individual monuments or sets of a few stones depicting one event and only a few people and places. The multiplicity of Early Urban stage stone monuments may reflect a pluralistic, open government.

The Ballplayers of Dainzú. A third corpus of carved stones, at the site of Dainzú, depicts ballplayers in dramatic, dynamic positions, as if they were making spectacular or difficult plays. Most are shown facing right with a ball in their right hand and wearing a special costume or uniform and protective gear. Some may be specific individuals designated by symbols: carved on the rock outcrops on the hill above the site are representations of helmets or heads (possibly severed from their bodies) with glyphs on them.

The ballplayers are found in the wall of a platform, Building A, that was probably constructed in Period II or Transition II-IIIa. Some of the carved stones are broken, so they originally may have been placed in an earlier wall, presumably built during Late Period I or Period II. This would also be the earliest date so far for the ballgame in Oaxaca.

Interspersed among the ballplayers in the wall are a few stones that have calendrical dates and show priests making offerings. Perhaps these images indicate days and ceremonies related to the ballgame, although the stones may derive from some other context.

The Dainzú stones also manifest the pattern of multiple individuals. One person, however, is distinguished from the other players. He stands upright on a place glyph, facing the others. He is more corpulent and appears to be a leader, pointing authoritatively to the players below him. The ballgame was important in various regions of Oaxaca; why it was so strongly emphasized at Dainzú is unknown.

Early Urban Stage Monuments in Other Regions

While not as numerous as in the Valley of Oaxaca, Early Urban stage carved stone monuments are known from several sites in the Mixteca Alta. At Huamelulpan, carvings including calendrical dates are evident on the corners of some large platforms. A lizard motif carved on one stone is perhaps a local symbol for place.

Monument 1 at Yucuita is a free-standing stone carved on two sides. A possible hill or cave glyph appears and within it, on one side, is a head wearing a mouth mask reminiscent of urns from Huamelulpan. Two other symbols — a circle with three horizontally placed dots, and something flying or floating in the air, perhaps a bat or butterfly — appear several times on the stone.

Carved stones from Diquiyú include cylindrical columns with personages carved on them. Plain columns occur at Monte Negro and Monte Albán in Early Urban times.

Glyphs indicating dates appear below a lizard carved on a large platform corner at Huamelulpan.

Symbols and Religion

Religion is an elusive area of archaeological inquiry because it involves beliefs not directly expressed in material objects. One source of information on pre-Hispanic religion in Oaxaca and elsewhere is information gathered in the early Colonial period by priests from native informants. Sixteenth-century documents include terms such as god of lightning, god of the hunters; god of hell, supreme or infinite god, and so forth. However, since Spanish priests' preconceived ideas undoubtedly colored the way they interpreted informants' reports, the meaning of the term "god" requires clarification. Belief in a god, several gods, or in some kind of supernatural beings is characteristic of most religions. We would like to know what people believed, and what deities may have been worshiped in Urban stage Oaxaca.

Ritual activities sometimes do leave archaeological remains which in turn may provide clues to religious beliefs. Mortuary rituals were particularly important in pre-Hispanic Oaxaca: ceramic urns, often deposited as funerary offerings or used in other ritual contexts, may be one of the best reflections of religion in the archaeological record.

Ceramic urns usually consist of a cylindrical vase adorned on one side by a human or part-human, part-animal figure with face, arms, torso, hands, legs, and feet modeled in clay and stuck onto the vase. The figure often displays an elaborate headdress, a mask, distinctive clothing, and symbols or glyphs. Urns are especially characteristic of the Zapotec area (the Valley of Oaxaca and surrounding mountains) and are also found in the Mixteca Alta and Baja. They first appear at the beginning of the Urban stage and are manifestations of people using symbols to reinforce their power.

Effigy braziers and vessels appear at the beginning of the Urban stage and are forerunners of urns. Most effigy vessels are bottles or jars with a human face and sometimes arms and legs attached to the exterior. Effigy braziers are cylindrical or hourglass-shaped vessels with a flat interior platform and eyes, ears, nose, mouth, and headdress modeled on the exterior. Braziers functioned as portable stoves holding live coals for heating, cooking, or ritual fires. (Pronged braziers have spikes rising up from the flat platform to support a cooking vessel.)

Two Late Urban stage Zapotec style ceramic urns representing Cocijo. The urn on the left is from San Juan Luvina, Macuiltianguis, Ixtlán, in the mountains north of the Valley of Oaxaca. The urn on the right is from Burial 55 at Fábrica San José in the Valley of Oaxaca.

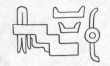

The god Cocijo shown left, in profile; and right, full face. Cocijo's image is often depicted on urns.

Some of the earliest glyphs in Urban stage Oaxaca appear in the center of the headdresses on effigy vessels and braziers, an early association of humans, partly supernatural beings, and symbols.

By Late Period I, gray ceramic urns were in use at urban centers in the Valley of Oaxaca and the Mixteca. Their distribution suggests that certain religious beliefs were held in common at least by the elite in these regions.

Zapotec urns, as well as effigy vessels and braziers, from Periods I and II, depict beings that combine human and animal attributes. Arms and legs look more or less human, while human and animal characteristics merge in the head and face. Period III urns usually show clearly the human face and appendages such as arms, legs, and hands. Personages are often depicted wearing elements such as bead necklaces, feathered headdresses, and circular earspools of the kind high-status individuals would have worn. Some urns, depicting people without symbolic regalia, have been found as "companions" placed next to the more elaborate urns.

Deities Some urns can be grouped on the basis of recurrent symbolic elements. In their study of Zapotec urns, Alfonso Caso and Ignacio Bernal refer to these as gods and goddesses. For example, one common class of urns is said to represent Cocijo, the Rain God (*cocijo* means lightning in Zapotec). Others are said to depict the God with the Helmet of a Wide-Billed Bird, the God with a Serpent Mask, the Bat God, and Goddess 2-J who wears what Caso called Glyph J.

Zapotec urns may represent powers or gods just as the images of saints or a painting of Jesus in a church do. Urns probably functioned as symbols, not as objects of worship in themselves. Some urns

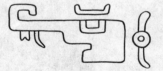

Of the common Period III deities, one is the Wide-Billed Bird, left above. A crocodile-like being, below, is another. The circle behind each creature's head in profile, is an earspool.

represent leaders or priests who have taken on special powers. By wearing a mask, the individual depicted on the urn impersonates extrahuman forces. The Zapotecs may have venerated and respected certain spirits and forces, communicating with them by means of an image of a man accompanied by appropriate symbols. Particular symbols or sets of symbols may have represented certain powers, deities, or gods, and may have been invoked during specific seasons, events, or ceremonies; thus some images and sets of symbols appear repeatedly.

In Late Period I a being with a distinctive down-turned human mouth (sometimes referred to as an Olmec-style mouth) is represented. This may be an early version of Cocijo. Several Period II urns from San José Mogote exhibit a mouth mask consisting of canine teeth and incisors. This, too, may be an early version of Cocijo.

In Period III at least three common and standardized beings are represented. One is Cocijo, distinguished by several features: squared-off frames around the eyes; a mask covering the nose and mouth with forked serpent tongue and a pair of canine teeth and incisors; the U-shaped Glyph C in the headdress; and frequently a pectoral on the chest suspended from a necklace.

A second Period III creature is the Wide-Billed Bird, often represented simply by the wide, down-curved beak. This being also has a distinctive rectangular eye. The Wide-Billed Bird appears in many contexts: as a mask on urns, as the jaws-of-the-sky motif, and sometimes adorning a place glyph.

A third Period III deity, a crocodile-like being with exposed gums and an up-curled snout or nose, also occurs in many contexts.

Little is known about beliefs surrounding these deities, but their ubiquitous appearance indicates great importance in Zapotec life. Often they are represented as abstract symbols (just an eye, beak, or snout) analogous to the way the cross is used as a symbol in the Christian church. The wearer of the symbol was imbued with its power.

Elite Appropriation of Symbols and History

Period IIIb-IV (A.D. 500-750) saw a great flourishing of Zapotec art, symbols, and writing. The Zapotec elite monopolized use of symbols and products of artistic craftsmen. Representations of deities usually appear in association with the elite, suggesting that high-status people used religion to reinforce their own power. Art and writing were no longer emphasized in public works but instead generally restricted to the private and personal use of the elite. In Early Urban times history and symbols were communal as shown, for example, by the danzantes and the Mound J slabs at Monte Albán. In Late Urban times at Monte Albán only a few carved monuments with glyphs were exhibited in public spaces. The stelae at the corners of the South Platform are among these few examples but, as Javier Urcid has pointed out, the stones were originally placed in a group forming a scene (of perhaps prisoners and a leader). The size of the carvings does imply public viewing, though perhaps in a restricted area. The function of this group of carvings may have been one of intimidation rather than commemoration.

On the other hand, exquisitely crafted materials are found in high-status residences and associated tombs. The images represent members of elite families while the symbols presumably refer to their names and perhaps their accomplishments. History and symbols were thus taken over by the elite; symbols were used for private glorification and to emphasize personal relations and power. History became particularized and transformed into private narratives of specific elite families. Late Urban elite history was expressed in several media.

Stuccoed sculptures. Friezes around the residential patio and portraits above the doorway of Tomb 6 at Lambityeco represent male and female heads of an elite residence. Emphasis on both males and females, undoubtedly married couples, suggests that kinship and lineage affiliation were reckoned through both lines. This pattern is also reflected in carved stone slabs described below, and in the occurrence of both male and female skeletal remains in some elite tombs. A fabulous stuccoed sculpture over the doorway of Tomb 5 at Cerro de la Campana (Huijazoo) depicts a bird emerging from the mouth of a crocodile-like deity. The sculpture denotes a Zapotec noble, perhaps the personage for whom the tomb was built, named 10 Crocodilia "Dove's Head".

Carved stone door jambs are present in Tomb 5 at Huijazoo and in tombs at the nearby site of Reyes Etla. They depict personages, sometimes framed by a place glyph and sky band, who may be nobles or guardians of individuals related to the dead. Some wear elaborate feathered headdresses and hold spears or staffs of office.

Painted murals occur on the walls of Tombs 103, 104, 105, 112, and 125 at Monte Albán, Tomb 11 at Lambityeco, and Tomb 5 at Huijazoo. They depict both male and female personages—probably

Stela 6 from Monte Albán, Period III. One of the "prisoner" stelae, it formed part of one corner of the South Platform. The man has his arms bound behind his back. Year sign and year bearer (deer) appear at upper left.

Portrait heads modeled in stucco over the entrance to Tomb 6 at Lambityeco of an elite couple, presumably members of the family who inhabited the house where the tomb is found. The images include their calendrical names — Lord 1 Earthquake and Lady 10 J.

members of elite families, their relatives, and perhaps their retainers. Possible supernatural beings—deities, perhaps guardians of the dead— are also shown.

Carved stone slabs. Finely carved rectangular slabs, usually no larger than one meter tall by 50 centimeters wide, depict scenes with elite personages. Some are divided into two or three separate panels relating a sequence of scenes. Rites of passage such as births, presentations of newborns, and marriages are common themes. Most scenes include a principal male and female figure with their names indicated by glyphs. The slabs are like books showing historical events in the family. Although most are from unknown context, small size and fine detail of the carvings indicate they were kept and viewed privately, in a tomb or residence. This was confirmed by the discovery of an exquisite slab in Tomb 5 at Cerro de la Campana (Huijazoo).

ETHNIC AND LINGUISTIC DIVERSITY

The rise of urban centers accelerated the formation of distinct ethnic and linguistic groups. Population increase is one factor that promoted cultural and linguistic diversity. As in the Village stage, major populations were concentrated in fertile valleys. In the Urban stage, however, groups expanded out from these valleys to less productive mountainous areas. Several regions of Oaxaca where Village stage occupations were sparse or are not yet documented have major Urban stage occupations—parts of the Mixteca Baja, the Zapotec Sierra, the Lower Río Verde area, the Chinantla, and the Mixe region. Some of these regions undoubtedly had Village stage settlements but the Urban stage populations were larger and the sites more dispersed.

Glottochronological analysis indicates three changes within the Otomangue language family during Early Urban times around 500 B.C. to 400 B.C., contemporaneous with the emergence of the first urban centers. Within the Mixtecan branch, Mixtec and Cuicatec separated, within the Popolocan branch, Mazatec separated from Ixcatec-Popoloca-Chocho, and within the Zapotecan branch, Chatino separated from Zapotec. These changes may all have been stimulated by the establishment of urban centers.

The centripetal effect of each local urban center is a second factor that promoted cultural and linguistic diversity. Village stage economic, social, and ceremonial activities had two foci—the domestic group and the village community. By adding a third focus, namely, the local urban center, a centripetal effect was created which led to spatial separation among groups. Simply in physical terms, the population in a small valley, for example, would have had much more interaction with the nearby local center than with communities linked to other centers. Thus the urban centers functioned as focal points for the generation and propagation of new styles and cultural patterns. Groups that were in conflict at a local level may have moved away, leading to settlement of some new areas and possibly the linguistic separations suggested by glottochronological evidence.

Competition and conflict are a third factor that may have led to linguistic and cultural diversity. Linguistic evidence also attests to changes within the Otomangue family in Late Urban times. Ixcatec separated from Popoloca-Chocho around A.D. 700; however, the areas occupied by these groups are practically unknown archaeologically so we lack data to evaluate a possible linguistic-archaeological correlation. At approximately A.D. 500 or A.D. 600, three languages—Chinantec, Mazatec, and Zapotec—underwent internal differentiation. This may reflect population growth and local conflict. In other words, as populations increased, no single regional center dominated or coordinated political and economic activities, and so local dialects developed.

Despite the conditions promoting diversity, Urban stage groups did not develop in isolation. Interregional contact through trade continued, as in the Village stage, and in Late Urban times elite groups in different regions probably established alliances through political agreements and intermarriage. Through the mechanisms of trade and alliances, groups in distinct regions had access to nonlocal goods and became aware of cultural innovations developed by others. Thus the two processes of diversity and unity were in play.

Regional Characteristics

The archaeological record of the Urban stage in Oaxaca reflects regional diversity in material objects—especially ceramics, which are the most common type of artifact found. The Urban stage is more fully documented than the Village stage, partly because there were larger populations and consequently more sites. Nevertheless, several regions, including some that undoubtedly had many inhabitants, such as the Mixe area and the Chinantla, remain practically undocumented.

Zapotec Region It is not surprising that Monte Albán, the largest city in pre-Hispanic Oaxaca, arose in the area with the largest expanse of flat, cultivable land in the southern Mexican highlands. The Early Urban population of the Valley of Oaxaca (at about 100 B.C.) may be estimated at 50,000 people and 700 communities. Monte Albán was the dominant center and uniquely large with 10,000 inhabitants or 20 percent of the valley's population. By Late Urban times (Period IIIb-IV) the valley population had increased to 100,000 inhabitants distributed in 1,000 communities. Monte Albán was still the principal city, with about 25,000 inhabitants, though some of the second-level centers (Huijazoo, Lambityeco, and others) may have competed with Monte Albán for political power, maintaining some degree of economic independence.

The Valley Zapotec (as compared to the Mountain Zapotec) influenced many groups in other regions of Oaxaca. Although evidence for what some have described as a militaristic, imperial state is flimsy at best, the Zapotecs did expand out from Monte Albán and the valley beginning in Early Urban times. The salt-producing site of Hierve el Agua in the mountains about 60 kilometers (by air) east of Monte Albán may have been controlled, if not occupied, by Zapotecs. Other Zapotec sites founded in the Urban stage were Cerro Iglesia at Atepec in the mountains 50 km. north of Monte Albán, Ixtepeji el Viejo in the same region about 30 km. north of Monte Albán, El Guexe in Miahuatlán 80 km. south of Monte Albán, and Yucuiní at Tepantepec in the mountains about 17 km. west of Monte Albán. These sites represent initial colonization of the Zapotec Sierra and the Miahuatlán Valley area (both are still major Zapotec subregions), as well as the mountains bordering the west side of the Valley of Oaxaca.

In Early Urban times these new settlements had incised gray pottery of the kind common in the Valley of Oaxaca. In Late Urban times they had many elements in common with valley communities such as gray ceramic urns, handled incense burners used in funerary ceremonies, rectangular tombs, the temple-patio-altar ritual precinct, and Zapotec-style carved stone monuments.

The distribution of Suchilquitongo bowls provides a good example of interregional contact. These bowls, made near Monte Albán, are found in sites as far away as the Mixteca Baja, the Mixteca Alta, the Cañada, and the Tehuacán Valley in Puebla. The precise mechanism of exchange is not known; they may have been distributed by traders or they could have been passed along from village to village without face-to-face contact of groups from different regions. Assuming that the bowls were used for the same specialized purpose—as pottery mortars for preparing sauces—outside the Valley of Oaxaca as within it, then their wide distribution means that culinary innovations which apparently originated at Monte Albán spread throughout highland Oaxaca.

Another type of interregional relation is suggested by the gray pottery decorated with incised designs that occurs in most areas of Oaxaca in Early Urban times. Most of it was locally made, so clearly the technique of its production was widely known and practiced at this time. However, there were many variations in combinations of forms and designs, and they differed from region to region.

A fascinating manifestation of interregional interaction was discovered by archaeologists excavating in the ancient city of Teotihuacan in the Basin of Mexico when they uncovered a residential section with pottery, a tomb, urns, and a carved stone, all in Zapotec style. Although they dubbed it the "Oaxaca

OAXACA

PRINCIPAL CITIES AND TOWNS, ARCHAEOLOGICAL SITES,
AND MAIN HIGHWAYS

STATE
OF
PUEBLA

TEHUACAN

TEOTITLAN

HUAUTLA

Cerro de las Minas

HUAJUAPAN

CUICATLAN

COIXTLAHUACA

Diquiyú

Yucuñudahui

Yucuita

Huamelulpan

NOCHIXTLAN

TLAXIACO

Monte Negro

Cerro de la Campana

PUTLA

San José Mogote

Yagul

OAXACA

Monte Albán

Dainzú

Lambityeco

STATE
OF
GUERRERO

Zaachila

OCOTLAN

EJUTLA

PINOTEPA
NACIONAL

JAMILTEPEC

MIAHUATLAN

Río Verde

TUTUTEPEC

PUERTO
ESCONDIDO

PACIFIC OCEAN

PUERTO ANGEL

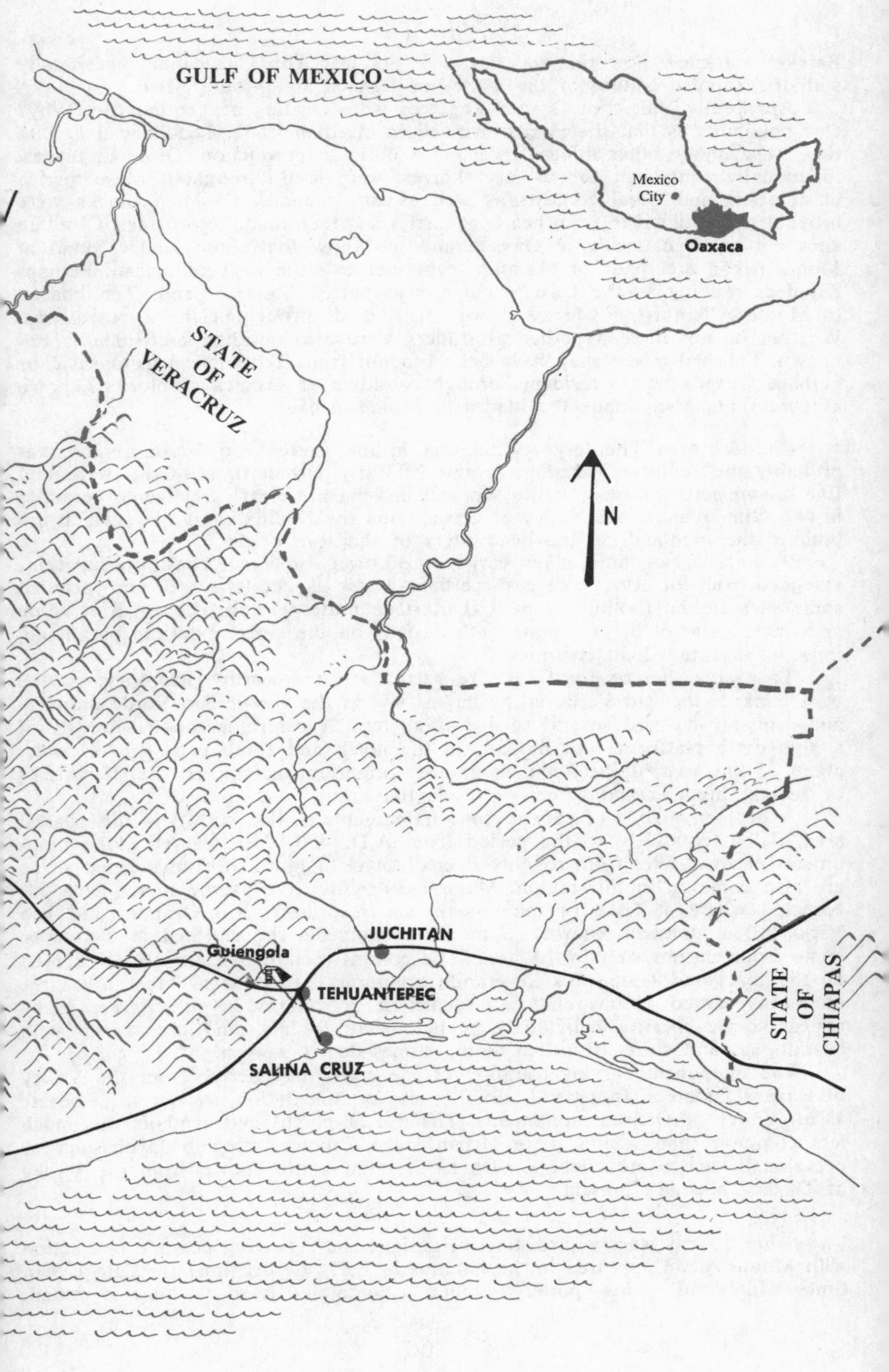

GULF OF MEXICO

Mexico City

Oaxaca

STATE OF VERACRUZ

N

STATE OF CHIAPAS

Guiengola

JUCHITAN

TEHUANTEPEC

SALINA CRUZ

Barrio," we know now that the ties were not just with Oaxaca but specifically with the Zapotec culture of the Valley of Oaxaca and Monte Albán.

Apparently Valley of Oaxaca Zapotecs were residing at Teotihuacan. Why? One possibility is that they were involved in obsidian trade. Teotihuacan at that time was, among other things, a center of obsidian production. Obsidian blades, functionally equivalent to our steel knives, were used throughout Mesoamerica in domestic and ritual contexts as well as for weapons. Obsidian blocks were brought to Teotihuacan from nearby quarries and then made into blades. Obsidian does not occur naturally in Oaxaca and we know that some blades found at Monte Albán are made of obsidian from sources close to Teotihuacan. Perhaps Zapotecs residing in the Oaxaca barrio transported obsidian from Teotihuacan to Monte Albán from whence it was distributed throughout the Zapotec area. Whether or not these hypothetical traders were also obsidian craftsmen is unknown. Finished blades may have been brought from Teotihuacan to Oaxaca, or perhaps Oaxaca barrio residents brought obsidian to Oaxaca in blocks (known as cores) and then made the blades at Monte Albán.

Chatino Area The large occupation in the Lower Río Verde region was probably the center of Chatino groups in Early Urban times. Gray ware and fine brown pottery with graphite slip and incising are clearly related to ceramics in two other regions, the Valley of Oaxaca and the Nochixtlán Valley, which are both in the highlands at the headwaters of the Río Verde.

By Late Urban times, if not earlier, the Lower Río Verde coastal occupations extended from the Río Verde east, perhaps as far as Puerto Angel, and included some sites in the foothills. Late Urban stage pottery in the Lower Río Verde area includes a lot of gray ware with designs on the vessel exteriors paralleling those of Monte Albán ceramics.

Two large sites on the Coast are particularly noteworthy. Río Viejo on the west bank of the Río Verde is the largest site in the Lower Río Verde drainage and probably covered several square kilometers. A central acropolis consists of a high earth platform with mounds at the north and south ends. Río Grande, about 35 km. east of Río Viejo, is another important unexplored site. It consists of several mounds and extensive residential areas.

A distinctive style of carved stone monuments is also known in this coastal area, dated tentatively to the period from A.D. 400 - 750. Carved stone monuments occur at sites from roughly Puerto Angel to Jamiltepec; unadorned stelae are also common in this region. Major sites with carved stone monuments are Nopala (where at least 14 monuments are recorded), Río Grande, and Río Viejo (10 monuments known). Some 15 monuments concentrated in Tututepec come from various sites in the area. The coastal monuments are usually carved on the black-and-white-speckled granite common in that area. Most are large monoliths carved in bas-relief and depicting personages in full figure. Many appear to be specific individuals, perhaps elite leaders, and are shown with headdresses and staffs of office. Some stones depict women.

The monument carving tradition of the coast may derive from the Valley of Oaxaca Zapotecs. In general, clothing and ornamentation are not so elaborate as on Valley of Oaxaca monuments. The use of glyphs and symbols was much less common than among Late Urban stage Zapotecs, though glyphs appear occasionally and some symbols, such as the flint knife, known from the Valley of Oaxaca also are present.

Isthmus Gray ware with distinctive designs and reflecting possible interaction with Monte Albán appeared in the Isthmus in Early Urban times; in Late Urban times white and yellow pottery similar to ceramics from Chiapas is found.

Right, stela from Río Manzo. Left, an *hacha* or axe. These hatchet-like stones with human faces carved on the thin edge probably had ceremonial functions. Their geographic distribution is similar to the thin stelae and both may be part of the same cultural tradition.

The Isthmus was presumably occupied primarily by Mixezoque speakers from the Village stage through Late Urban times although, as today, it may have been an area where territories of many groups intersected.

Tall, thin carved stones with representations of men have been found in the Isthmus and near the Oaxaca-Veracruz border; these may be Mixezoque cultural manifestations of Late Urban times. One large stela comes from La Ladrillera, a large Urban stage site in Juchitán; another comes from Río Manzo in the District of Choapan, one of the least documented archaeological regions in the entire state.

Mixteca Alta From Early Urban times cultural differences between the Mixteca Alta and the Valley of Oaxaca are clear. For example, at 200 B.C. yellow and brown pottery predominated at Yucuita while gray and cream wares were most common at Monte Albán. Metates at Yucuita were small and decorated; at Monte Albán they were large and plain. Mortuary customs varied: at Yucuita there are narrow, rectangular tombs with multiple superimposed skeletons. At Monte Albán, however, burials generally consisted of only one individual; multiple interments sometimes occur in tombs but the skeletons are separate rather than piled on top of one another.

The Mixteca Alta, unlike the Valley of Oaxaca, consists of many separate valleys. In Early Urban times some diversity among these valleys was evident. For example, Yucuita in the Nochixtlán Valley and Cerro del Pedernal in the Coixtlahuaca Valley have distinctive bowls with corncob impressed bases that have not been reported elsewhere. Many urns were found at Huamelulpan but almost none at Yucuita; figurines representing humans with monster-like heads are common at Yucuita but absent at Huamelulpan.

In Late Urban times the Mixteca Alta remained distinct from other regions; for example, yellow and orange pottery including anular-base bowls were common. (Anular-base bowls have a ring of clay on the exterior of the base which serves as a support to prevent tipping.) Elite families there probably had direct links with other regions—for example, paintings occur on a wall of Tomb 1 at Yucuñudahui, as they do on some elite tombs at Monte Albán in the Valley of Oaxaca. However, the Yucuñudahui tomb has a large square main chamber—a shape distinctive to this part of the Mixteca Alta.

Mixteca Baja During Late Urban times the so-called Ñuiñe culture flourished in the Mixteca Baja. (*Ñuiñe* means "hot country" in Mixtec and is a name for the region.) Among the distinctive aspects of Ñuiñe culture are urns of orange or brown pottery with pedestal bases, decorative *grecas* (repetitive geometric designs) and scrolls or volutes; carved stones; and ceramics of a paste containing large chunks of mica derived from schist, a type of metamorphic rock common in the region. Orange pottery is common as are anular-base bowls, and both are still made today in the town of Silacayoapilla. Orange anular-base bowls relate stylistically to ceramics from Teotihuacan and the Central Mexican urban centers, but are local products. At Cerro de las Minas in Huajuapan there are stone platforms with overlapping projecting stones on the corners, resembling log-cabin construction.

Stone monuments found at sites around Huajuapan and Tequixtepec were probably carved between A.D. 350 - 750. The largest single corpus consists of some 35 stones from Tequixtepec. Many are rectangular blocks of black basalt and come from sites in the hills around the town. Each stone seems to be a complete unit in itself, displaying glyphs that indicate a date and a place together with an event or a person. Numerals are indicated by bars and dots and some glyphs are similar to those known from the Zapotec region, suggesting that the writing system derived from the Zapotecs. Even so, certain glyphs and the design compositions are distinctive and show local innovation and development. At Cerro de las Minas the use of carved rectangular slabs of soft white stone placed in panels is common in the Late Urban stage.

Cañada The first substantial occupation of the Cañada emerged in Early Urban times. Distinctive patterns of grouped dwellings with cobblestone foundations appeared and gray ware with incised designs peculiar to the region was common. No carved stones and little or no monumental architecture are documented for Early Urban times. These archaeological data support the linguistic data that indicate a split in the Mixtecan branch of Otomangue into Mixtec and Cuicatec at this time. The Mixteca region underwent great population growth and increase in cultural complexity at this time while the Cañada remained relatively sparsely populated.

In Late Urban times fortified hilltop and mountainslope sites appeared. The site of Quiotepec at the juncture of the Río Salado and the Río Grande has been partially excavated and was evidently an important site in Early as well as Late Urban times. Another large site, Tepeusila, situated high above the floor of the canyon, also may have been the center of a local polity. Undecorated gray pottery was common in Late Urban times.

Mixe Region A looted site at Juquila Mixes yielded a lot of brown pottery but little gray ware; a few figurines were found, similar in form but not paste to those from the Valley of Oaxaca. The Late Urban period has not been

Left, a Ñuiñe urn from a tomb at Santiago Chilixtlahuaca in the Mixteca Baja. Below, Stone 1 from Tequixtepec shows a glyph in a circular frame with the number six or 11 (one or two bars and a dot) below it, indicating a calendrical date. The hand grasping the club depicts an action — perhaps conquest or sacrifice — directed toward a man fallen over a place glyph. Although direct evidence of human sacrifice is rare in Urban stage Oaxaca, conflict, capture, and possibly sacrifice are frequent themes on carved stone monuments.

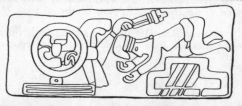

documented, and this region in general is so poorly known in archaeological terms that it is difficult to describe relations with other regions.

Chinantla Late Urban occupations are known from San Juan Luvina in the highlands and Ayotzintepec in the lowlands. Ayotzintepec also probably had an Early Urban stage occupation. Other sites are known in the Valle Nacional area, where environmental conditions excellent for agriculture imply that the Lower Chinantla was an important area for pre-Hispanic occupation. Presumably the ancestors of the Chinantecs lived here during the Village stage, although without more archaeological study the nature of the sites and their possible ethnic affiliation will remain hypothetical.

Mazatec Sierra The use of Blade Cave near Huautla in Early Urban times may reflect initial colonization of the Mazatec highlands and correlate with the linguistic data that suggest that Mazatec separated from Ixcatec-Popoloca-Chocho around 500 - 400 B.C. Late Urban stage sites occur at Huautla (a double tomb), **Eloxochitlán** (vessels and a carved human mandible), and perhaps at San José Tenango (stone-constructed tombs). A large site at Ayautla next to the Río Santo Domingo appears to have a large central plaza and mounds. It would be interesting to try to determine the ethnic affiliation of this site since it is on the river connecting the Tehuacán Valley and the Cañada with the Chinantla region.

Portion of a polychrome mural from Tomb 104 Monte Albán. It shows a priest with extended hand, carrying in the other hand a copal bag (?). Three deities and accompanying dates are depicted in front of him.

THE END OF THE URBAN STAGE

The end of the Urban stage, around A.D. 750, is best documented in the Valley of Oaxaca. After a remarkably long occupation spanning some 1,200 years, the city of Monte Albán was abandoned and construction at the site ceased.

The demise of Monte Albán as a functioning city marked the transition to a new economic and political organization. Why this change took place is another intriguing question for archaeological study.

One hypothesis is that the tribute system fell apart and that people moved away to places with easier access to resources. What may have happened is this: Monte Albán's high mountaintop setting meant that as the city grew, basic products necessary to sustain the inhabitants became scarcer. Firewood, originally available on Monte Albán's slopes, was depleted at an early stage in the city's development. Water from springs on the hillsides was adequate at first, but in later times, even with the large reservoir to the northwest, people had to walk all the way down to the Río Atoyac for water. Alluvial farm land, originally abundant, became relatively scarce as the city grew, and terrace soils used for kitchen gardens were also depleted. To compensate for these scarcities, Monte Albán pressured its dependent communities for more goods in tribute. Tributary communities, however, refused to participate, and since Monte Albán lacked the power to enforce its demands, the system collapsed.

Archaeological evidence suggests that political organization at Monte Albán in Period IIIb-IV was indeed fragile. Only four or five Period IIIb-IV elite palaces are known; the elite seems to have constituted a disproportionately small percentage of the population. Some simple Period IIIb-IV households were producing pottery, which might indicate that specialists in other communities were no longer supplying Monte Albán's residents with ceramics.

This interpretation of political breakdown and depletion of resources fits what is known about Monte Albán but leaves unexplained why other Period IIIb-IV (A.D. 500-750) sites in the Valley of Oaxaca as well as in other regions—Teotihuacan in the Basin of Mexico and various centers in the Mixteca Alta, for example—declined dramatically in population or were abandoned at about the same time. Monte Albán was not an isolated case: some pan-regional phenomenon, probably widespread climatic change and drought, or possibly an epidemic, may have been a causal factor. Whatever it was, any such catastrophe remains to be demonstrated.

Exactly what happened in Oaxaca after the demise of Monte Albán and other urban centers is also unclear. There is a period of several centuries from about A.D. 750 to A.D. 1250 for which the archaeological data are problematical, as we shall see in the next chapter. It is evident, however, from shifts in settlement locations and from changes in material culture that the political organization was modified. The end of the Urban stage heralded another transformation in pre-Hispanic Oaxaca, and within a few centuries the threads of urban civilization were to be woven into a new organizational fabric—the city-states.

THE CITY-STATE STAGE:
A.D. 750 - 1521

Scene from the Codex Nuttall characteristic of City-State stage pictographic writing which contrasts with the more abstract, ideographic writing of the previous Urban stage. Here the famous Lord 8 Deer is undergoing the nose-piercing ceremony in which he received a nose ornament signifying high status.

After the abandonment of Monte Albán, Yucuñudahui, and the other urban centers, a new political organization came into being—the City-State. Functioning as independent kingdoms, each city-state had a population of several thousand people distributed among various settlements, within a recognized territory.

The term "city-state" is used here to convey not only the idea that small cities were the principal communities, but also the existence of state-level government. By definition, a state is an autonomous political unit encompassing several communities within a well-defined territory, has centralized government, a social and political hierarchy, and the power to tax (or exact tribute from) its members. We know through archaeological and documentary evidence that all these characteristics were present in this final stage of pre-Hispanic Oaxaca—the last centuries before the Spanish Conquest—hence the characterization of this period as the "City-State stage" is appropriate.

Each city-state had a principal town that functioned as the political capital and seat of the governing family as well as a religious and market center. Second-level towns, administered by lower-echelon nobility, served market and ceremonial functions on a smaller scale. Some commoners lived in principal or second-level towns, while others lived in hamlets and dispersed settlements in the rural areas. In contrast to the previous Urban stage, relatively little effort was dedicated to public, community construction.

Population of the Oaxaca region reached an estimated maximum of 1.5 to 2.5 million people in the City-State stage, roughly three times larger than the Urban stage population. The results of Bruce Byland's surface survey in the Tamazulapan Valley in the Mixteca Alta exemplify this increase: from the Urban to the City-State stage, the number of archaeological sites doubled from 90 to 180 and the estimated population more than tripled from 6,000 to 20,000.

Social stratification was sharply defined during the City-State stage. Class distinctions were hereditary. The nobles were divided into a relatively small group of governing royalty and a group of second-level administrators. The two groups were related through kinship and

71

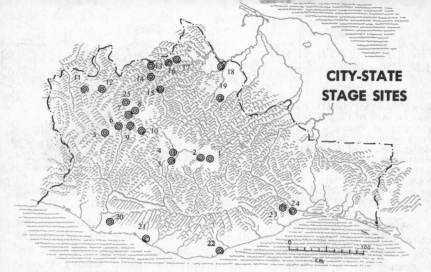

CITY-STATE STAGE SITES

1. Mitla, 2. Yagul, 3. Zaachila, 4. Mogotes de Bartolano, Xoxocotlán, 5. Tlaxiaco, 6. Achiutla, 7. Yanhuitlán, 8. Chachoapan, 9. Tilantongo, 10. Jaltepec, 11. Tonalá, 12. Cerro del Sombrerito, Huajuapan, 13. Cerro Hidalgo and others, Teotitlán, 14. Tecomavaca, 15. Pueblo Viejo or Iglesia Vieja, Cuicatlán, 16. Huautla. 17. San José Tenango, 18. Tuxtepec, 19. Ayotzintepec, 20. Tututepec, 21. Puerto Escondido, 22. Huatulco, 23. Guiengola, 24. Cerro Padre López, 25. Inguiteria.

sometimes marriage, and noble families formed political and marriage alliances linking different city-states. On the lower end of the social scale were the commoners, including laborers and farmers. Some were part-time specialists who made pottery, wove cloth, and produced palm mats and baskets, and other goods for domestic use. Some commoners owned land while others worked as serfs on nobles' land. There were slaves in some city-states—usually war captives.

Mitla, Yagul, and Zaachila are the best known archaeological sites of the City-State stage in Oaxaca. Each functioned as the center of a city-state in the Valley of Oaxaca. These sites reflect an emphasis on elite residences rather than large public structures.

Settlement locations changed in this period compared to the Urban stage. Principal towns were situated in the valleys, on low slopes next to major rivers and extensive alluvial lands as in the Village stage, rather than on hilltops as in the Urban stage. In the mountainous regions main sites were on slopes or ridges. Hamlets and isolated households were established in previously unoccupied piedmont and mountain areas—farmers apparently now had varieties of corn that rendered hillside cultivation viable. Stable political organization may have been another factor that permitted people to live in dispersed settlements.

Nevertheless, conflicts did arise. The large hilltop centers of the Urban stage combined urban and defensive functions, but in the City-State stage these functions were separated. The main communities were situated in relatively indefensible positions but protected by fortresses

72

constructed on high points above the city. Fortresses provided vantage points and would have offered temporary refuge, especially for women and children, during raids on the town. They usually lacked permanent structures and storage facilities for food and water that would have permitted sustained occupation. Examples include the fortress on the cliffs overlooking the palaces at Yagul and the hilltop fortress a few kilometers west of the main buildings at Mitla. Monte Albán was apparently used as a fortress in late City-State times, probably by people living around Xoxocotlán: a wall built over the north edge of the South Platform is part of an enclosed, defensible area.

Domestic Life

Domestic life continued essentially unchanged. As in the Urban stage, the size and elaborateness of residences mirrored status hierarchy. Most dwellings were simple rectangular wattle-and-daub or adobe houses with stone foundations and thatch roofs, like the Village stage houses of many centuries earlier. The nuclear family persisted as the basic domestic group. Elite families lived in elaborate multiroomed palaces with stuccoed walls and floors. Average households in different regions of Oaxaca had similar inventories of pottery vessels: thin comales (like those made and used for cooking tortillas today), simple hemispherical bowls for serving food, thin-walled water jars, and cooking pots of relatively gritty, coarse texture.

Fine gray pottery, used for serving vessels, has been found in many regions of Oaxaca. A particularly common form is a bowl with three effigy supports or feet resembling, for example, bat heads, deer hooves, eagle-serpent heads, or iguana heads, depending on the region.

Most people ate simply—corn, beans, squash, chile, avocado, greens, and wild plants including fruits. Clothing was also simple: loincloths for men, and skirts and shawls for women. Some people wore fiber sandals. Tools included implements of stone and bone for cutting, scraping, and pounding, and wooden digging sticks for planting corn and weeding the cornfield.

Nobles had more elaborate residences, food, and clothing. Craft specialization and the tribute system were highly developed and commoners had to contribute goods and/or labor to the local noble family. Market systems were well-organized and some non-local goods such as obsidian were widely available. However, metal objects, polychrome pottery, ornaments of shell and semiprecious stones, and other sophisticated craft items were restricted to the nobility.

Mortuary Practices

Mortuary customs differed from region to region, but the tradition of burying the dead in or near the residence generally persisted. Commoners were usually buried in simple graves, often with one or two ceramic vessels as offerings. In the Mixteca Alta, for example, burials are often found in small subsurface pits. In the limestone country of

Stucco sculptures from Tomb 1 at Zaachila. On the wall of the antechamber, the owl symbolized night and death. Two figures from the main chamber walls — Death and 5 Flower.

the Mazatec Sierra and the Chinantla, the dead were often placed in caves, usually simply on the cave floor accompanied by a vessel or two as offerings.

While elite individuals were generally interred in tombs with relatively elaborate offerings, burial treatment varied greatly. For example, Tombs 1 and 2 at Zaachila lie below the patio of a palace, in a pattern similar to that of Period IIIb-IV at Monte Albán. Both Zaachila tombs yielded remarkable offerings of polychrome pottery and many other luxury objects, and Tomb 1 is noteworthy for the stuccoed relief sculptures on its walls.

The most famous elite burial of the City-State stage is Monte Albán's Tomb 7, an example of a burial not associated with a residence. Its contents have been called among the richest treasures of the New World because of the gold and silver ornaments (3.598 kilograms of gold in all), carved bones, obsidian earspools, and other finely worked objects found there. The osteological remains represent bones of 12 to 14 different individuals. The tomb structure was built many centuries before the interment, when Monte Albán was still flourishing. The offerings and the bones (evidently those of ancestors) constitute the legacy of an elite family that probably lived somewhere in the Valley of Oaxaca, perhaps at Xoxocotlán, but not at Monte Albán which by then was uninhabited. Exactly why these remains were carried up to Monte Albán and buried is open to question.

Elsewhere at Monte Albán simple burials of the City-State stage have been discovered. These remains have been found in seated position, suggesting that they may have been carried up to the site in bundles, similar to the way burials are represented in the codices. Sometimes fragments of a comal and serving vessels are found on the surface near the burials, as if the funeral ceremony and interment had involved partaking of a ritual meal. The people who performed these last rites apparently came from villages near the valley floor since no late residences are found up on Monte Albán. They probably considered Monte Albán a sacred place, perhaps an ancestral home.

The noble corpse is shown seated and wrapped in the Mixtec style of burial, as represented in the Bodley Codex.

74

The archaeological record of the City-State stage is complemented and complicated by events related to the Spanish Conquest. In A.D. 1519 Spaniards arrived in what is now Mexico. On August 13, 1521, after a three months' siege, Hernán Cortés and his soldiers finally defeated the Aztecs and took control of their capital, Tenochtitlan, now Mexico City. A few months later Spanish soldiers entered the Valley of Oaxaca, and during the next several years they established settlements and initiated commercial activities in various parts of what is now the state of Oaxaca.

Some Spanish towns were new settlements; in other instances existing communities of the City-State stage became the nuclei for new centers under Spanish authority. In either case a plaza, or *zócalo,* was set up and streets were laid out in a grid pattern on the Spanish model. Thus some major pre-Hispanic sites are found within the limits of present-day towns: some examples are Mitla and Zaachila in the Valley of Oaxaca, Teotitlán and Cuicatlán in the Cañada, Tilantongo and Yanhuitlán in the Mixteca, and Tututepec on the Coast.

Frequently, to facilitate administration, Spanish overlords imposed a policy of *congregación* that obliged indigenous people to leave their rural homesteads and move to (or "congregate in") the towns. Abandoned residences, and in some cases entire communities, fell into ruin and became archaeological sites. They are often still in relatively good states of preservation since, although roofs and walls collapsed, most house foundations, burials, and refuse deposits were not destroyed by later occupations. Today near many towns in Oaxaca it is common to find a place the local people call *pueblo viejo,* or old town; this usually refers to a late pre-Hispanic settlement occupied just before the communities were relocated by the Spaniards.

Since the congregación took place some years after the Conquest, European objects often appear in the earlier rural sites—ceramics, glass, metal tools, and bones of domestic animals such as goats, sheep, pigs, and cattle brought to the New World by the Spaniards. With the introduction of Christianity, mortuary customs changed and the dead were buried in cemeteries instead of next to the residences. Symbolic elements also changed: traditional religious symbols were no longer painted on pottery but were replaced by abstract, geometric designs.

CITY-STATE ORIGINS

The City-State stage can be divided into early and late periods. Virtually all archaeological evidence assigned to the City-State stage, such as the buildings at Mitla and Yagul, the contents of Monte Albán's Tomb 7, and artifacts such as polychrome pottery, metal ornaments, and the codices, corresponds to the late period, from approximately A.D. 1250 to the Conquest. The early period, from about A.D. 750 to A.D. 1250, has not been clearly documented archaeologically and

Carved deer (?) bone from the Cueva de Tenango. Geometric designs, particularly the circles with dots, may represent counts. Perhaps a handle; feathers, or some other organic material, were tied through the perforations at one end.

seems to be a gap in the sequence following the Urban stage. Thus questions arise as to whether there was continuity in peoples, languages, and cultural elements between the Urban stage and the City-State stage. Was there much movement and shifting around of linguistic and ethnic groups in Oaxaca, and did new groups appear? Although definitive answers will be obtained only through future research, enough similarities do seem to exist between the Late Urban and the City-State stages to support a claim of general cultural continuity between these periods.

For example, in the Valley of Oaxaca the following continuities are evident:

* The house with closed layout (a patio surrounded by rooms) appears at Monte Albán and Lambityeco in Late Urban times and in the palaces at Mitla, Yagul, and Zaachila in the City-State stage.

* The importance and power of the elite family is evident in both stages. In Late Urban times this is manifested (aside from residences) in carved slabs and stucco friezes showing elite personages, while in the City-State stage family histories are narrated in codices.

* The painting style of the codices is anticipated in Late Urban stage polychrome tomb murals in the Valley of Oaxaca.

* The use of grecas and carved bones appears in Late Urban times in the Valley of Oaxaca and these elements are depicted later in the codices of the City-State stage.

Left, grecas, one type of Mesoamerican symbol, appear in many media. Some are called "stepped fret." Right, grecas in stone at Mitla.

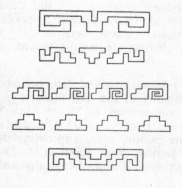

These continuities are general and could have been passed on by any or various groups present in Oaxaca during the Urban stage. However, in some specific aspects of culture there is no continuity from Late Urban to City-State times: the best example is Zapotec writing which ends in the Late Urban stage. The writing system used later in the City-State stage and manifested in the codices may have its origins in earlier writing systems; that is, some artistic conventions—the depiction of people and places and the elements used to represent them—are common to both systems. But the glyphs, which are culturally and linguistically distinctive elements of Zapotec writing, are absent in the codices.

If there is continuity between the stages, why does archaeological evidence seem to be lacking for the early part cf the City-State stage, between A.D. 750 - 1250? One possibility is that the Urban stage ended with a drastic decline in population, perhaps due to drought and agricultural failure. Small groups may have lived on in various regions, maintaining the same language, traditions, and customs, but living in simple communities without large buildings or other elaborate constructions. The specifics of Zapotec writing may have been lost with population decline.

Some new groups probably did enter Oaxaca during Early City-State times, specifically the Huave, Chontal, and Nahuatl speakers. In general, however, the city-states developed from roots established in the Urban stage.

PICTURE-MANUSCRIPTS AND WRITTEN DOCUMENTS

Pre-Hispanic and Colonial documents complement and enrich the archaeological record of the City-State stage. By late pre-Hispanic times picture writing was used throughout Mesoamerica to record historical information and ritual procedures. The Spaniards introduced script writing and the alphabet, and in the first decades after the Conquest many documents that registered aspects of pre-Hispanic history and culture were elaborated in Spanish and occasionally in native languages. Many early Colonial documents show a combination of the pictorial and European writing traditions. So for the City-State stage the archaeological record actually includes documented historical events and people, as the following examples show.

Codices

At the time of the Conquest picture manuscripts existed in the hands of many leaders of city-states in Oaxaca. A few were obtained by Spaniards in the first year or two after contact and sent to Europe where they found their way into private collections and libraries. Some others were fortuitously conserved in Mexico. But most such manuscripts in Oaxaca and elsewhere in Mesoamerica were destroyed by Spanish priests during the early years of Spanish rule. Among the few surviving manuscripts from pre-Conquest Mesoamerica are eight codices, or screenfold "books" painted on deerskin coated with white lime, from the Mixteca regions of Oaxaca, known as the codices Nuttall, Bodley, Selden, Vienna, Colombino, Becker I and II, and Sánchez Solis.

The Codex Nuttall, for example, consists of 47 pages, each about 19 centimeters high and 25.5 centimeters wide, and most of them painted on both sides. Unfolded, the codex measures over 11 meters long.

These so-called Mixtec codices deal with genealogical and historical matters and show personages and places; all but two include information about the Mixtec ruler 8 Deer "Tiger Claw." (In City-State times individuals were often named for their birthdate in the ritual calendar, thus the name *8 Deer*. They also had a personal name referring to some characteristic, in this case "Tiger Claw.")

Lord 8 Deer "Tiger Claw". Lord 8 Deer supposedly was born in Tilantongo and, according to Alfonso Caso's reckonings, lived from A.D. 1011 to A.D. 1063. (Some experts would advance these dates by a generation or two.) He became a powerful political leader, conquering and subjugating many towns. He apparently united and consolidated a large area of the Mixtec-speaking region, becoming ruler of the city-states of Tilantongo in the Mixteca Alta and Tututepec on the Coast.

Since the archaeological record for the period from A.D. 750 to A.D. 1250 is poorly documented and since the codices that have survived were painted after A.D. 1300, questions arise about the historicity of 8 Deer's life. How much is history and how much is legend? We may never know how many of his accomplishments were real and how many were attributed to him through recounting from generation to generation, with embellishments and exaggerations.

Some ongoing research may help answer this question. In 1985, Bruce Byland and John Pohl began surveying the Tilantongo and Jaltepec areas of the Mixteca Alta; they have located archaeological sites that seem to correspond to places depicted in the codices Nuttall and Selden. Surprisingly, however, the sites date back to Late Urban times rather than to the City-State stage when the existing codices were actually painted. This means that the preserved codices may be copies of much older (and now lost) painted documents. A remarkably long historical tradition is thus represented and the past evidently had great importance.

The Borgia Group of Codices. Another important group of codices, known as the Borgia group, includes the Codex Borgia, the Féjérvary Mayer, the Laud, the Cospi, and the Vaticanus B. These codices deal with ritual and divination; they do not show place names, dates or historical personages, and thus they differ from the Mixtec codices. Although they resemble the Mixtec codices in painting style, no one knows with certainty where they come from. Likely possibilities are the Mixteca Alta, the Chinantla, the Mazatec region of Oaxaca, the Tehuacán Valley, or the Tlaxcala area. Of course, codices, like books, are portable, so they could have been painted in one place and then carried to another.

Maps and Lienzos

Maps and lienzos are post-Conquest documents painted on rectangles of paper or cloth. They usually depict a town and its territorial limits, and sometimes a genealogical sequence of ruling families. Maps and lienzos often functioned as legal documents. (*Lienzo* is linen, hemp, or cotton cloth; early Colonial-period maps drawn or painted on cloth are often called lienzos, while those on paper or canvas are usually called maps.) Sixteenth-century maps and lienzos often include dates, place signs, and other elements in native pictorial style, while later examples tend to show more European influence. One group of several lienzos in similar style comes from the Coixtlahuaca Valley; several others are known from the Mixteca de la Costa and from the Zapotec Sierra.

The Lienzo de Guevea. The Lienzo de Guevea is a large, rectangular painted cloth from the town of Guevea de Humboldt in the Isthmus of Tehuantepec and was studied initially by the German scholar Eduard Seler. The original lienzo, painted in 1540, is known only from two later copies, which apparently differ somewhat from the original.

In the center of the upper half of the lienzo is the glyph for the town of Guevea with symbols of surrounding towns indicating territorial limits. The lower half deals with a succession of rulers. At the bottom is the place sign of Zaachila, the late Zapotec capital in the Valley of Oaxaca, and above it, in a vertical column, are various rulers. These depictions imply that the late Zapotec rulers in the Isthmus came from the royal lineage of Zaachila.

Tree-birth scene from the Vienna Codex. The tree grows from the head of a woman face down on a feathered plain. Two priests perforate the tree with instruments. A man is being "born" at the top of the tree; the woman has already emerged.

Large buildings made of stone slabs with mud mortar and covered with a thin coat of white stucco are still standing at the late Zapotec site of Guiengola near Tehuantepec. Monumental buildings here, including the stepped platforms with slightly slanted walls, are similar to those constructed by Zapotecs in the Valley of Oaxaca 1,000 years earlier.

Among the rulers depicted are Cocijoeza, the Zapotec ruler of Zaachila and Tehuantepec who came to power in 1482, and his son Cocijopij who in 1518 was given the rulership of Tehuantepec. Cocijopij's mother was the Aztec princess Pelaxillo, or Cotton Tuft. After the Conquest, Cocijopij took the name Juan Cortés and continued ruling. He died in 1563, in Nejapa, a town halfway between the Isthmus and the Valley of Oaxaca. Cocijoeza died in 1529 in Zaachila. Thus the lienzo brackets the Conquest, showing personages from both before and after the arrival of the Spaniards.

Written Documents

During the early years of Spanish rule, many documents were written in Spanish (and some in native languages) that dealt with administrative matters such as land disputes, claims to titles, accusations of idolatry, commercial transactions, and other legal matters. Many have been preserved in church and government archives. These documents, studied by ethnohistorians and experts in Colonial history, often refer to native communities and indigenous customs.

Another group of documents consists of the writings of the Spanish priests who arrived in Mexico after the Conquest to begin evangelization and conversion of the Indians. Some of them lived in native communities, learned indigenous languages and customs, and recorded them in publications. The Dominican order was active in the Oaxaca region and several significant studies were written by Dominican priests. Among them are Fray Juan de Córdoba's study of Zapotec language, and studies of Mixtec by Fray Antonio de los Reyes and Fray Francisco de Alvarado. Published in the late 1500s, they not only record the languages in use at the time of the Conquest but also define many words important for understanding the social order and religious beliefs of the period.

Valuable data also appear in the *Relaciones Geográficas,* prepared in the late 1500s at the request of the Spanish crown in answer to a questionnaire about the native communities and their resources.

Certain chronicles and histories written after the Conquest, sometimes based on informants' observations, are also helpful sources of information, although in some cases they are of questionable reliability. Such is the case, for example, with Fray Francisco Burgoa's two major works, *Palestra historial* and *Geográfica descripción,* written in the 17th century, while he served the Dominican order in Oaxaca more than 100 years after the Conquest. These books describe in great detail the history of the Dominicans in Oaxaca and also contain information on the history and customs of Zapotecs, Mixtecs and other groups interspersed with expressions of Burgoa's evangelizing fervor. In these writings it is difficult to distinguish between legend, hearsay, and Burgoa's own observations.

Certain myths and legends, including some mentioned by Burgoa, figure prominently in the oral traditions of some present-day indigenous communities in Oaxaca and undoubtedly have pre-Hispanic origins. An example is the Mixtec tree-birth story which appears in the codices, on carved bones from Tomb 7, in historical accounts, and is still told today in various forms. It relates that the Mixtec noble lineages (of the City-State stage) were born from trees in the town of Apoala on the eastern edge of the Mixteca Alta. Apoala is in a unique, beautiful, and fertile valley surrounded on three sides by cliffs. A river comes out of the base of the cliffs, runs through the valley, drops off in a waterfall, and flows down to the Cañada. If there had been a general drought and population decline in the highlands, Apoala might have been one place where small groups lived on, which in turn might have given rise to the origin myth.

CRAFT SPECIALIZATION

Technological and artistic sophistication in the crafts characterized the City-State stage. While a variety of materials were worked into domestic and luxury products, with the exception of obsidian we have little direct information on where these artifacts were made, who made them, and how they were distributed. Perishable items such as cotton and maguey-fiber textiles and animal-skin and feather robes must have been important along with the pottery, stone, and metal objects that are more commonly available for study.

Polychrome Pottery

Polychrome or multicolored pottery existed in all regions of Oaxaca in the City-State stage, and the several distinct varieties were undoubtedly made by different groups. (The term "Mixtec polychrome," some-

A polychrome bowl in re
black and white from the ca
at San José Tenango in tl
Mazatec area.

times applied to polychrome pottery in general, is misleading since it
obscures the fact that many groups made and used this kind of ceramics.)

In Oaxaca, ovens and workshops for the production of polychrome
pottery have yet to be found and studied. However, the differences
among varieties are clear enough to rule out the possibility that one
group of potters produced all of it. Since the varieties of polychrome
share some attributes such as the use of fine paste, application of a
white and/or orange slip, and the uses of red, black, and other colors
for decoration, it is evident that knowledge of certain *techniques* existed
in different regions and that local specialists produced their own versions.

A list of some varieties of polychrome known in Oaxaca includes
the following:

Cholula polychrome. Polychrome pottery was produced in abundance in
Cholula, state of Puebla. Vessel walls are relatively thick; surfaces tend to be
waxy, even shiny; geometric and codex-style motifs are common as decoration.
Pottery of this type was probably imported to the Mixteca, accounting for its
sometimes being called Cholula-Mixteca. Some varieties within this group may
have been produced in Oaxaca.

Chinantla polychrome. Thin-walled vessels of yellow-orange paste commonly
feature fine line decoration in geometric motifs. The vertical-necked pot with
three supports is a common form. This ware has been found at Ayotzintepec
and other sites in the Chinantla and at San José Tenango and Huautla in the
Mazatec Sierra. It was evidently imported to the latter region.

Southern Isthmus polychrome. This is characterized by medium-thick vessel
walls, yellow-orange paste color, geometric designs in medium-wide lines, and
white slip often left exposed (undecorated) in large areas. It has been found in
the Tehuantepec area.

Río Verde-Tututepec polychrome. These medium to thin-walled vessels were
made with paste containing tiny mica platelets, probably derived from Río Verde
clays. Graphite decoration is common, as are intricate, fine line designs that
include codex-style motifs.

Tenango polychrome. Characteristics are thick walls and yellow to buff slip
with white, black, and red decoration. Hemispherical bowls are common; this
ware does not occur in the common polychrome forms of pots and bowls with
tripod supports. Tenango polychrome may have been made in northern Oaxaca
or near the Oaxaca-Veracruz border; it has been found in San José Tenango.

Xoxocotlán polychrome. Found in and around Xoxocotlán in the Valley of
Oaxaca, this pottery is of dark red paste, medium-thick walls, white slip, and
simple geometric decoration. Undecorated vessels of the same paste also exist.

Turquoise Mosaics

Objects adorned with turquoise mosaic inlays have been found in several regions of Oaxaca and other parts of Central and Southern Mesoamerica. Turquoise was apparently obtained from northern Mexico and perhaps as far away as the southwestern United States. It was cut into small, thin pieces and, along with other kinds of blue and green stone and shell, placed in mosaic fashion in designs over the exterior surface of wood and bone objects. Circular shields and wooden masks were among the most common type of artifacts to be so decorated.

In Tomb 7 at Monte Albán a human skull with mosaic inlays was found, and fragments of disks and masks were found in Tomb 1 at Zaachila. A circular wooden shield with inlays was recovered from the Cueva de Tenango. Evidently highly prized and obviously made by master craftsmen, these objects were probably exchanged among the elite.

Obsidian

Obsidian outcrops have not been found in Oaxaca, but most households in Oaxaca had access to obsidian blades used for cutting tasks. It is known that much of the green obsidian used in Oaxaca in the City-State stage came from the Sierra de las Navajas in the state of Hidalgo. Gray and black obsidian is also common and came from Veracruz and the state of Mexico.

Obsidian workshops of the City-State stage have been found in Oaxaca at Mitla in the Valley of Oaxaca; at Achiutla and Tejupan in the Mixteca Alta; and at Teotitlán in the Cañada. The kinds and amount of debris found in the workshops indicate that obsidian was brought in as large, roughly prepared blocks or as macro-cores with the cortex already trimmed off. Trimming would have saved on weight during transport since the cortex was later discarded anyway. Once at the workshop, final core preparation took place and blade production began. Blades were struck off the core until the raw material from the original block or core was used up

Since blade production is a specialized skill, the question of who made the blades arises. Interestingly, the workshops at Achiutla, Mitla, and Tejupan are on or beyond the outskirts of the pre-Hispanic settlements; this might imply the presence of outsiders. If local people were the obsidian workers, one would expect the workshops to have been in their houses. If nonlocal craftsmen produced obsidian blades outside a town, observers would have been unlikely.

In addition to household implements, obsidian in the City-State stage was also used for earspools, made by abrading and polishing the raw material to a delicate thinness. These are found with high-status burials such as Tomb 7 at Monte Albán and Tombs 1 and 2 at Zaachila. Obsidian earspools were perhaps produced by specialists in Central Mexico and then traded along with other luxury goods to elite families in other regions.

Metal

Metal implements and ornaments appear in Oaxaca for the first time during the City-State stage. Among the most common artifacts are spherical, hollow gold beads, T-shaped copper axes, *cascabeles* or tinklers (similar to sleigh bells) of copper and silver, solid copper axes, and rings made of thin strips and wires of copper and sometimes silver. Within each artifact category there is striking uniformity even though the artifacts are found in places separated by many kilometers. This implies that they were made by specialists as standard items.

Gold, silver, and copper occur naturally in many parts of Oaxaca but no direct evidence of pre-Hispanic metallurgy has been found in the state.

According to documentary evidence, the Tarascans who lived around Lake Pátzcuaro and Lake Chapala in Western Mexico were renowned for metalworking during the City-State stage. Many of the standardized metal items found in Oaxaca and elsewhere may have been produced by Tarascan specialists and then widely traded among the elite.

A few metal objects, however, such as the pectoral and rings found in Tomb 7 at Monte Albán, exhibit dates, representations of gods or personages, and other complex elements rather than simple, geometric designs. These must have been produced by craftsmen who understood the meanings of the symbols they used or had seen similar examples. If they are pan-Mesoamerican symbols, then the artifacts may have been produced by any specialist, but if the designs are regionally specific then the artisan would have had to have been familiar with local traditions.

Copper axes. Thick copper axeheads, evidently used as tools or weapons, are found occasionally in Oaxaca. Distinct from these are the so-called T-shaped copper axes, said to have been used as money or currency in late pre-Hispanic times. T-shaped copper axes, which appear toward the end of the City-State stage, are shaped like the end of a spade. They are only about one or two millimeters thick and have slightly raised edges along the shaft. They usually lack evidence of sharpening or use on the curved distal end, and since they are generally

Heavier axehead at left was evidently a tool; T-shaped axes were much thinner. Copper was also used to make bells. Gold ring is from tomb at Ayotzintepec.

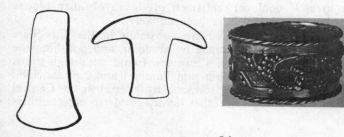

not found broken or discarded in domestic refuse, they appear not to have been used as tools.

T-shaped axes are sometimes found in caches of several dozen nearly identical specimens, as if they had been buried in a bundle or a bag. Only rarely do they occur in Oaxaca as grave goods or tomb offerings, in contrast to other metal artifacts and ornaments. Thus the T-shaped axes appear to have been neither implements nor ornaments. Perhaps this was the form in which copper was handled as a tribute commodity. If there were standard sizes and weights, as appears to be the case, the axes may actually have functioned as standards of exchange or a kind of currency.

RELIGION, RITUAL, AND SYMBOLS

A group of symbols appeared throughout Mesoamerica during the late part of the City-State stage. Similar motifs expressed in a distinctive style occur in various media—codices, ceramics, carved bone, mural paintings, and others. Some common motifs, as noted by H.B. Nicholson in various articles, are:

* Representations of birds, animals, insects, flowers, eagles, jaguars, and especially serpents, including the feathered serpent and the fire serpent.

* Representations of celestial phenomena—sun, moon, stars, Venus.

* Elements related to war, death, and sacrifice—skull and crossed bones; warriors holding circular shields, arrows, or darts; and banners, shown with downy feathers signifying sacrifice.

* The stepped-fret, conch shell in cross-section, and other motifs.

* The 20 signs of the ritual calendar. (The 260-day ritual calendar is manifested in the codices with a somewhat different system of notation than in the Urban stage. The year is indicated by the so-called A-O year sign, resembling a capital A with interlaced O, and all numerals are represented by dots; the bar representing five is not used.)

The motifs listed above appear in a relatively uniform style, involving, as Nicholson has pointed out, "geometric precision," vivid colors, recognizable though not necessarily realistic portrayal, and cartoon-like standardized postures. This combination of motifs and style has also been called "codex-style" and "Mixteca-Puebla" style. The latter designation is misleading since the Puebla and Mixteca areas were not necessarily the places of origin of the style nor do they have priority as centers of its expression. Another term, "Postclassic religious style," suggested by Michael E. Smith and Cynthia Heath-Smith, correctly conveys the idea that the motifs were more than simple decorative elements, although their religious aspect is not clear. The designation "pan-Mesoamerican symbol system" encompasses the idea of widespread occurrence of symbols without implying anything about shared religious beliefs.

PAN-MESOAMERICAN SYMBOLS

FLOWER

FEATHERS

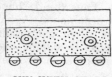

SKY WITH STARS

FLINT KNIFE

SUN/DAY - STARS/NIGHT

Pan-Mesoamerican ubiquity suggests acceptance and acknowledgment of the symbols by many distinct ethnic and linguistic groups. This is reminiscent of the Olmec horizon two thousand years earlier when certain symbolic motifs appeared among numerous groups throughout Mesoamerica. In the City-State stage, common motifs would have been seen and presumably understood by all members of society. Presence of these motifs implies to some degree a common cosmovision or view of the human being and his situation in the universe. But, as in the case of the Olmec horizon, a wide range of beliefs may underlie the symbols. For example, the cross appears as a symbol for Christianity in many parts of the world, although varying beliefs are subsumed by that faith. In parallel fashion, there are regional variations in the outward expression of the late pan-Mesoamerican symbol system, and presumably in the beliefs expressed by the motifs.

The consolidation of elements of the symbol system and its spread throughout Mesoamerica were probably linked to and facilitated by interactions among the noble class. Alliances and tribute relations would have served as channels for exchanging information as well as goods. Thus the cultural diversity promoted by population growth and social and geographic isolation was counteracted by unification due to links among elite groups plus the Aztec domination of tribute networks in the last half-century before the Conquest.

In a sense, the City-State stage can be seen as the reverse of the Village stage. Now, instead of all men being subject to the gods, the gods were subject to a few men. As we saw earlier, the appropriation of the gods by a few people began at the end of the Urban stage—at Lambityeco, for example, where gods represented by stucco masks are depicted in the patio of a high-status residence. Later examples are the representations of the gods on the jewels from Tomb 7. Here the gods are reduced to small, symbolic expressions on luxury items that could be carried around as the personal property of the ruling elite.

There is some archaeological evidence in Oaxaca of local cults or group-specific beliefs. For example, stone heads are common in some regions—the Coixtlahuaca area and around Tlaxiaco and Tilantongo (but not in the Nochixtlán Valley) in the Mixteca Alta. The heads

Ñuhus or earth spirits dwell in and "own" the earth, and are often shown in the codices as little men with protruding teeth, lumpy heads and limbless bodies. Above, from the Vienna Codex, two ñuhus are associated with two halves of the solar disc, perhaps indicating sunrise and sunset. Right, a stone ñuhu from Tilantongo.

from Tlaxiaco and Tilantongo resemble Tlaloc, the Central Mexican rain god, as well as the ñuhu, or earth spirits, of the Mixtec codices. In the Mixe region, stone figurines found near Tlahuitoltepec show complete bodies.

Another dimension of religious and ritual activity took place at the household level in the City-State stage. Personal ritual, which began back in the Village stage, continued to be an important part of life for the average person. Common practices were rites involving curing or petitions for rain or fertility. Today in Oaxaca such rites are often performed at hilltop shrines under the supervision of a ritual specialist, or healer. As in the past, pungent copal (resin from the copal tree) may be burned and offerings presented—flowers, cigarettes, and food and drink, including alcoholic beverages. Small birds, chickens, and turkeys are sometimes sacrificed.

Blood-letting often accompanied rituals, apparently involving fertility, rites of passage, and petitions to the gods for health and well-being. This ancient practice is documented archaeologically as early as the Village stage. A special stingray spine perforator was used to draw one's blood (a maguey spine or other sharp instrument would have served as well) from ear, tongue, or genitals. The blood was then collected as an offering. Miniature vessels of the City-State stage found in the Nochixtlán Valley may have held the blood in such rituals.

Caves

Caves played an important role in the ritual and ceremonial life of some Oaxaca groups, especially in City-State times. Traditionally, caves provided access to the underworld; they are entrances where earth spirits appear on the surface, then return to their abodes. Since these spirits may be harmful, many people consider caves dangerous.

Caves (deep caverns as distinct from simple overhangs or rock-shelters) are especially common natural features in the limestone mountains that run from the southern Isthmus diagonally across the northern part of the state of Oaxaca toward Puebla, encompassing much of the Mixe, Chinantec, and Mazatec territories. Except for parts of the Mixteca, the areas south of this line have metamorphic rock exposed on the surface and are generally lacking in caves. Many limestone caves are deep caverns with underground rivers inaccessible to all but expert speleologists. Some of the world's deepest caves have been recorded around Huautla in the Mazatec region.

Archaeological evidence shows that caves were entered and used in pre-Hispanic times. Some caves containing archaeological remains are difficult of access and must have been visited only by skilled climbers using ropes. However, most caves with evidence of pre-Hispanic use are horizontal and could have been entered by almost anyone using a pine torch for light.

Cueva de Ejutla, a dry cave in the mountains between the Valley of Oaxaca and the Cañada, was used for burying the dead. Cell-like constructions of stone masonry built against its walls apparently served as individual burial crypts. Unfortunately, the cave was looted years ago, but archaeological salvage work recovered fragments of palm mat and sandals, fibers used for tying bundles, and fragments of two artifacts indicative of at least one high-status burial—a piece of woven cotton cloth with a design painted in blue and a fragment of a wooden mask with turquoise mosaic inlays. Bodies were probably wrapped as seated mummy-bundles; the mask may have been placed over an individual's face. Cuicatec or Mixtec speakers may have used the Cueva de Ejutla.

Blade Cave. Several caves with archaeological remains are known in the Mazatec-speaking area around Huautla. Pottery vessels from about the time of Christ (Early Urban stage) found in Blade Cave are the earliest documented occupation in the Mazatec Sierra. Blade Cave was also used in City-State times, and the human bones, bifacially flaked chert knives (mistakenly called blades by the speleologists who found and named the cave), obsidian blades, and beads of stone, shell, and coral found there may come from this later visitation.

Artifacts in Blade Cave were evidently left during both periods as offerings, but we don't know what rituals were performed. The human bones may simply indicate use of the cave as a cemetery, as appears to be the case in some other Huautla caves. However, the chert knives are similar to those used by the Aztecs for performing human sacrifices, and the obsidian blades may have been used for ritual blood-letting. The beads and some vessels, still in place, are clustered around an area where water collects in a pond on the cave floor. Surface water

Obsidian blades are long narrow flakes with parallel sides, each blade made by a single blow. The edges are sharper than those of a steel knife though not so durable. Chert knives are made by removing numerous flakes from both surfaces of a preform to produce a thin, leaf-shaped implement also with sharp edges often hafted to a wooden handle.

Petroglyph of a whale visible on a cliff about 60 kilometers from the Pacific Ocean. There are many petroglyphs, among them a squid, at this locale — near a spring, evidently one of the few permanent water sources in this arid, mountainous part of the Isthmus. Both the location of the petroglyphs and the marine motifs suggest the water source was an important place. Perhaps the petroglyphs record a visit by a coastal group, such as the Huave.

is virtually absent in the Mazatec regions since it immediately filters down into the porous limestone, so caves with pools may have been used and venerated as water sources.

Cueva de Tenango, also in the Mazatec Sierra, near the town of San José Tenango, contained a remarkable quantity and variety of artifacts from the City-State stage including more than 300 ceramic vessels of both utilitarian and elegant polychrome wares, hundreds of shell beads, imported manos and metates of black, gray, and red basalt, a wooden shield with turquoise mosaic inlay, ornaments of gold, silver, and copper, obsidian blades, a carved slate slab, animal bones with incised designs, and many other objects.

Two stone-masonry structures were possible high-status tombs and the obsidian blades may have been used for ritual blood-letting. Most of the human bones were placed around a small pool of water containing hundreds of shell beads and other personal adornments, again suggesting the possibility of offerings made in relation to water.

Human bones from the cave represent remains of 22 individuals of both sexes. There was one child under 10 years old, seven individuals between 10 and 17 years old, and 14 adults from 19 to 30 years of age. This is not a random sample of the population—children and older individuals are under-represented—and the question arises as to why these individuals were interred in the cave. Were they sacrificial victims? Whatever the answer, the Cueva de Tenango was clearly a ritual sanctuary of great importance and must have been entered numerous times for performance of rites.

PICTOGRAPHS AND PETROGLYPHS

Pictographs—paintings on rock walls, usually cliff faces—exist in many parts of Oaxaca. Lack of direct association with other archaeological materials makes them hard to date; most are probably from the City-State stage. Some of the simplest pictographs are hand prints made by placing a hand on the wall and painting around it, usually in red.

A pictograph on the cliff just to the east of the access road to the site of Yagul shows a greca design and above it a stick figure that appears to be a man. The motifs are painted in white over a red background.

Some magnificent multicolored (red, yellow, white, black) pictographs occur at Tonalá in the Mixteca Baja. They show spirals, apparently sun or shield symbols, and many other motifs. An elaborate, multicolored feathered-serpent pictograph occurs at a site in the Cañada.

Petroglyphs—designs pecked or incised into boulders or rock walls —also exist in many regions of Oaxaca and also are difficult to date for lack of association with other materials. Most examples in Oaxaca are probably from the Urban and City-State stages. Some petroglyphs simply show motifs incised on boulders and are not much different from carved stone monuments. In some cases designs are scattered, mixed, and sometimes superimposed, and appear to have been put on the rock at different times. Some petroglyphs are associated with springs, which may have been sacred places venerated during seasonal visits over many years.

THE AZTECS

The Aztecs came to the Basin of Mexico around A.D. 1250 and initially settled and worked as subjects of the flourishing city-states of Azcapotzalco and Culhuacán. In A.D. 1325 the Aztecs founded their own capital, Tenochtitlan, and sometime before A.D. 1440 defeated the last of their rivals and took political control in the area. At times during the subsequent 80 years up until the arrival of the Spaniards and under various emperors, the Aztecs conquered and subjugated groups outside the Basin of Mexico, establishing a wide-ranging tribute empire. A hierarchy of tribute control already existed in most regions and the Aztecs simply added another level, meaning that local leaders now had to turn over a portion of their collected goods to Tenochtitlan.

Political alliances between Aztec leaders and provincial governors were sometimes forged and consolidated through marriage alliances. For example, in order to settle a conflict, the Aztec king Ahuitzotl gave his daughter Pelaxillo to the Zapotec leader Cocijoeza. Through alliances provincial leaders became participants in extensive trade networks. Many special products, if not actually made in Tenochtitlan, were controlled by the Aztecs. Aztec trader-merchants carried goods (obsidian, metal, turquoise, and many others) from the capital to the provinces and returned with cacao, quetzal feathers, rubber, jaguar skins, and other exotic items as well as information. Thus both through force and peaceful establishment of alliances, the Aztecs created economic networks and links communicating diverse regions of Mesoamerica. Noble families in the provinces profited by obtaining goods as well as status through association with the Aztecs. Some such interrelationships apparently began long before the Aztecs, which would account for the widespread appearance in Mesoamerica of standardized

90

luxury goods as well as common stylistic and symbolic elements.

By the mid-15th century the Aztecs had made incursions into Oaxaca. City-states centered at Tlaxiaco (Mixtec) and at the site of Inguiteria near Coixtlahuaca (Chocho) were under Aztec domination, as were Teotitlán de Flores Magón (Popoloca or Mazatec) and Tuxtepec (Chinantec). Important trade routes from Central Mexico to the south passed through Teotitlán and Tuxtepec and then continued on to the Maya region, including the Yucatan Peninsula, the Soconusco on the Chiapas Coast, and Guatemala.

The city-states of the Valley of Oaxaca may have been disrupted by the pressure of Aztec domination of the Mixtec city-states. Post-Conquest documents indicate that some Mixtec groups settled in the Xoxocotlán-Zaachila area. This may have occurred sometime after A.D. 1450 though the dates are not certain. In the years just before the Conquest, conflicts erupted between Mixtecs and Zapotecs. Cocijoeza, the Zapotec leader of Zaachila, apparently fled to Tehuantepec on the Isthmus perhaps around A.D. 1500. The fighting ended with the arrival of the Spaniards.

After the Conquest, Nahuatl, the language spoken by the Aztecs, became a lingua franca for legal and administrative purposes in much of Mesoamerica. A Nahuatl name was used as the official designation for many towns. Most towns in Oaxaca are known today by their Nahuatl name preceded by a saint's name, although most also have names in the native language of the area. The name Mitla, for example, comes from the Nahuatl *Mictlan* which means place of the dead. The official name is San Pedro and San Pablo Mitla. In Zapotec, Mitla is called *Lyobaa,* which also means place of the dead.

Huaxyacac (Oaxaca City)

Historical sources relate that the Aztec emperor Ahuitzotl, who reigned from A.D. 1486 to A.D. 1502, established a garrison at Huaxyacac, now Oaxaca City,in order to exact tribute from the Valley Zapotecs. (The Aztec word *Huaxyacac* means at the point or nose of the *guaje,* the acacia tree commonly found on the piedmont slopes of the Valley of Oaxaca and which produces pods with edible seeds.) The garrison, presumed to have been comprised of Aztec administrative buildings, official residences, and ordinary houses, was supposedly located in the area of what is today the market just south of Oaxaca's main square.

Since no archaeological evidence of the garrison has been found (test excavations in the market might yield some evidence) the existence of the garrison remains questionable. The purported presence of an Aztec garrison in Oaxaca City may be based on a misinterpretation of the Spanish term *guarnición* which can mean either fortified structure or outpost, or simply a detachment or party of soldiers, with no implication of settlement. Such a group or guarnición may have passed through or temporarily occupied an area now within city limits. Whether they left archaeological traces or whether such traces would be recognizabl Aztec is doubtful.

The center of Oaxaca City is built on alluvium and would hav been inappropriate for pre-Hispanic settlement; flood waters from th Río Atoyac would have covered the area on occasions. In 1979 archaeo logists of the Centro Regional de Oaxaca excavated in the Alamed the plaza between the Main Post Office and the Cathedral. We hav also inspected many miscellaneous excavations in the city, especiall trenches opened for drains and underground cables. In the Alamed and elsewhere, there are about 1.5 to 3 meters of alluvium and/o post-Hispanic rubble — and sometimes an occasional pre-Hispani potsherd — but so far no evidence of a pre-Hispanic settlement.

Sites do exist, however, north of the Pan-American highway (Mexic 190) in piedmont areas that have recently become suburbs of the city For example, a Period V tomb was found in the INFONAVIT housin development just north of the Colonia Reforma, and Period I throug V occupations have turned up around the area of the Benito Juáre Autonomous State University medical school (formerly the Hacienda Aguilera) next to the river that comes from San Felipe del Agua.

ETHNIC AND LINGUISTIC GROUPS

Population increased substantially throughout Oaxaca during th City-State stage; archaeological remains are plentiful and even thoug many regions of the state have not yet been surveyed, ethnohistoric dat provide information on the distribution of ethnic and linguistic group at the time of the Conquest which, of course, marks the end of th City-State stage. The distribution of ethnic and linguistic groups ha remained generally the same in the years since the Conquest althoug indigenous groups were either displaced or assimilated by the colonizer in many areas desirable from an agricultural or commercial standpoin (for example, the central part of the Valley of Oaxaca, the Lowe Río Verde Valley, the Coast in general, and parts of the Isthmus).

One correlative of population growth and settlement expansion during City-State times was increase in linguistic diversity, especiall emergence of dialect variation within the major language groups.

Three of Oaxaca's 16 language groups may have moved into thei present areas during this stage, though only future research will deter mine whether local antecedents exist. These are Huave and Chonta on and near the Isthmus and Nahuatl in northern Oaxaca.

Archaeologists would like to know to what extent ethnic and lin guistic groups are manifested in the archaeological record. This ha to be determined empirically, from archaeological fieldwork and com parison of the data. We can, however, explain in theory why we woul expect evidence (potsherds, architectural styles, burial practices, an so forth) to vary among city-states.

As the basic political unit, the city-state defined the territory withir which economic interaction took place. Pottery and other object produced by artisans within a city-state would have been distributed primarily to people who participated in the markets controlled by the governing elite. Consequently, specific vessel forms and decorative elements, for example, would be used and discarded within a local territory. People within the same city-state would have had relatively more interaction with each other than with people in other, parallel political units. Thus language as well as customs—that is, house styles, burial practices, types of tools, ways of making pottery, and so forth—would be relatively similar within a city-state and distinct from those in other city-states. If interaction of distinct city-states happened most frequently among contiguous units that spoke the same language, then the distribution of artifacts and stylistic variables would correspond to ethnic and linguistic groups.

More study must be undertaken to test these possibilities and to see what kinds of archaeological remains are found in border areas between ethnic groups. We must also take into account goods that were exchanged among different groups and that would not correspond to local, intraterritorial distribution. An interesting example is a specific type of rectangular tripod metate made of black vesicular basalt and used with a long, thin mano. These have been found at Ayotzintepec in the Chinantla, at San José Tenango in the Mazateca, and at Cuicatlán in the Cañada—all areas where no naturally occurring basalt is found. These implements may come from somewhere in Veracruz, such as the Tuxtla Mountains, or perhaps, from the Mixteca Alta region around Yucuita where basalt outcrops are found. In any event, distribution of this style of mano and metate indicates links and exchange among groups in the northern part of Oaxaca and perhaps trade along the Río Grande in the Cañada and the Río Santo Domingo, which separates the Cuicatec from the Mazatec region.

Valley of Oaxaca

Patterns in the archaeological data reveal several subareas within the Valley of Oaxaca during the City-State stage. This variation may reflect presence of separate city-states, or the existence of different ethnic groups (Zapotecs and Mixtecs), or changes that occurred within the stage that spans nearly 800 years, from A.D. 750 to A.D. 1521.

Eastern area. This area, which includes Mitla, Yagul, and other sites with decorative mosaic grecas adorning tombs and buildings, extends from Xaaga on the east to Tlalixtac on the west where there is a tomb with greca panels over the doorway similar to those at Yagul. The panels and grecas derive from Late Urban stage Zapotec architecture and suggest that Zapotecs built these structures. The area is Zapotec today and presumably has been occupied by Zapotecs for millennia. John Paddock's ethnohistoric research suggests that Macuilxochitl and perhaps other towns may have been governed by Mixtec rulers during Late City-State times. It remains to be seen whether any archaeological evidence of Mixtec rulers can be detected.

Central area. According to ethnohistorian John Chance and based on John Paddock's studies of 16th-century documents, in Late City-State times Mixtecs occupied the central portion of the Valley of Oaxaca in a triangular area extending

from a Mixtec neighborhood in Zaachila northeast to San Andrés Huayapan an
west to Santa María Atzompa. Paddock estimates from 20,000 to 70,000 Mixtec
were present.

The principal town was at Cuilapan, and other Mixtec towns included Sant
Cruz Xoxocotlán, San Juan Chapultepec, and San Andrés and San Pedro Ixtla
huaca. The ruins of Monte Albán fell within this Mixtec domain. Mixtec an
Zapotec languages are no longer spoken in these towns but Mixtec is spoke
today in several mountain villages such as Santa María Peñoles, San Mate
Tepantepec, and Santiago Tlazoyaltepec just to the west of Monte Albán.

In Late Urban times this mountainous area was within the Zapotec spher
centered at Monte Albán. However, with the collapse and abandonment of Mont
Albán, the mountainous region as well as the central part of the Valley o
Oaxaca remained sparsely inhabited. Then during the City-State stage Mixtecs i
the Mixteca Alta expanded, perhaps eastward from the Nochixtlán Valley, even
tually occupying the mountains west of the Valley of Oaxaca and then movin
down into the valley.

The question of Mixtec occupation of the Valley of Oaxaca has long bee
debated among archaeologists. One extreme viewpoint holds that there was a
Mixtec invasion and conquest of the valley; the other extreme denies Mixte
presence. If the ethnohistorical evidence is valid, both extremes can be rule
out and we might expect to find distinctive cultural and material remains re
flecting some degree of Mixtec presence.

Until recently there were still a few Mixtec speakers in Cuilapan; the presen
lack of indigenous languages in the central part of the Valley of Oaxaca is no
surprising, however, since that area was the first to be acculturated by th
Spanish overlords, beginning early in the 16th century.

Archaeological evidence reflected in house types, burial patterns, and domesti
artifacts might reflect Mixtec presence. Unfortunately, except for the palace
at Mitla, Yagul, and Zaachila practically nothing is known about late pre-Hispani
house types in the Valley of Oaxaca. In the Mixteca Alta, late burials occur i
flexed position in subsurface pits; examples found at Monte Albán and Tierra
Largas could conceivably be Mixtec burials. Domestic artifacts do not shov
obvious links with the Mixteca Alta: pottery in the Mixteca is different fron
pottery in the Valley of Oaxaca. Two-tone gray bowls and gray bowls with three
effigy supports are common in the Valley of Oaxaca. Characteristic of the
Mixteca Alta are bowls with red-on-cream painted decorations, large ladles o
spoons, decorated miniature vessels, and handled incense burners with two sup
ports. The latter are all rare or absent in the central part of the Valley of Oaxaca

It is also possible that the Mixtecs in the central part of the Valley o
Oaxaca had distinctive pottery of their own. Tomb 1987-1 in Xoxocotlán containe

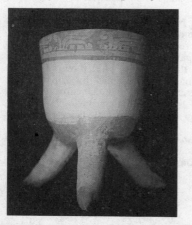

A distinctive variety of polychrome pottery characterized by reddish paste and
prominent use of white slip is found in
the Xoxocotlán area. Gray ware of the
same reddish paste is also found, and
these varieties of pottery may be limited
to a city-state centered at the site of
Mogotes de Bartolano on the south side
of the town of Xoxocotlán.

pottery that might support this hypothesis. It is made of fine dark-red paste, almost certainly locally produced. Some vessels are fired to a gray-black exterior color; others are oxidized and decorated as white-on-red and white-red-black-and-orange polychrome. This pottery has also been found at a late settlement at the southern base of Monte Albán. It could be interesting to determine whether the overall distribution of this ware corresponds to the area of supposed Mixtec occupation of the central Valley of Oaxaca.

The unexcavated archaeological site known as Mogotes de Bartolán is probably the best candidate in the Cuilapan-Xoxocotlán area for the principal town of a Mixtec city-state. Located on the southern outskirts of Xoxocotlán, it has two adobe mounds, one rectangular (probably a palace) and one tapered at the top (probably a temple). The mounds are separated by a large plaza.

Monte Albán's Tomb 7, Tombs 1 and 2 at Zaachila, and the palaces at Mitla have all been attributed at one time or another to Mixtecs. Some archaeologists have argued that polychrome pottery, architectural grecas at Mitla, codex-style paintings on the Mitla palace lintels, and other traits indicate Mixtec presence. It is important, however, not to confuse style with ethnic affiliation. Since all late pre-Hispanic groups participated in the pan-Mesoamerican symbol system, many design elements are not indicative of ethnic affiliation. Similarly, luxury goods widely distributed among elite groups in Late City-State times, are signs of high status but not indicators of ethnic identity. Until more is known about where such objects were made, who made them, and how distribution was controlled, we cannot assign them to any particular ethnic group. If the ethnohistoric data are correct, Monte Albán was within the Mixtec area of the central part of the Valley of Oaxaca; one could ascribe the bones and the treasure of Tomb 7 to Mixtecs simply on the basis of geographical location of the tomb.

Physical, osteological evidence might help identify the ethnic affiliation of the individuals in these tombs. If it could be shown from controlled samples that Mixtecs and Zapotecs had physical differences, then burials from different parts of the Valley of Oaxaca could be analyzed and shown to correspond to one of the two groups. However, intermarriage between Zapotec and Mixtec nobility might have obscured some possibly distinctive genetic patterns.

Etla Valley. Late pre-Hispanic archaeological data from this valley are complex. No large sites equivalent to Mitla and Zaachila are known that might have served as principal towns of city-states, but various tombs and burials have been salvaged and reflect wide variation. This is precisely what one would expect if portions of the valley had been occupied and/or controlled off and on by different groups—or if they had never been integrated for long under one group. The position of the Etla Valley adjacent to the Mixteca Alta may have meant that it was a buffer area separating major Zapotec from Mixtec centers.

At least three complexes of materials can be defined. One is documented by two tombs excavated near the town of Alemán. Tomb 1 was a rectangular stone-masonry construction containing bones of many individuals. Small conical cream-ware bowls and flat and circular greenstone ornaments were among the most prevalent grave goods. The other, Tomb 3, was essentially a concentration of bones with skulls piled up at one end, and all covered with stones. The same kind of cream-ware bowls and greenstone ornaments were found. Vessels similar to the Alemán examples are known from Santa Ana Yareni in the mountains north of the Etla Valley. Polychrome pottery was absent, so the Alemán tombs may belong to the early part of the City-State stage.

A second Etla Valley manifestation exists around Huitzo and Suchilquitongo and consists of rectangular tombs with carved or decorated lintels made of pinkish quarried and cut rock from Suchilquitongo. Pottery found in these tombs includes

Red-on-cream bowl from Yucuita, Natividad phase. Red-on-cream bowls are common during the City-State stage in the Mixteca Alta. Local variations occur; for example, design elements in the Nochixtlán Valley are distinct from those in the Coixtlahuaca Valley.

burnished red-on-cream which may be relatively early in the City-State stage. Gray tripod bowls have also been found in these tombs.

A third complex is represented by Tomb 1 at Barrio del Rosario, Huitzo. It has a distinctive shape: two rectangular rooms placed with their long axes perpendicular to the entrance. This is similar to Urban-stage tombs from the Nochixtlán Valley in the Mixteca so it may be Mixtec. (Tomb 1987-1 at Xoxocotlán had a similar rectangular shape which perhaps could indicate Mixtec affiliation.) The tomb lintel is painted and the offering included polychrome pottery and gold beads, placing the tomb chronologically in the Late City-State stage. Several burials in Mixtec-style pits were excavated near Tomb 1 in the Barrio del Rosario, Huitzo. Also, red-on-cream pottery, typical of the Mixteca Alta, is more common around Huitzo than other parts of the Etla Valley. So this Huitzo tomb and associated burials are good candidates for Mixtec presence in the Etla Valley.

The eastern portion of the Etla Valley, around San Pablo Etla, for example, may have been within the Valley Zapotec area. A salvaged tomb at San Pablo Etla contained gray bowls typical of the Late City-State stage in other parts of the Valley of Oaxaca.

The archaeological data, then, suggest a culturally complex situation in the Valley of Oaxaca during the last centuries before the Conquest. Some ceramics, burials, tombs, and sites around the base of Monte Albán (possibly including Tomb 7) may derive from Mixtec groups mentioned in historical documents. Zaachila and sites further from the center of the valley were occupied principally by Zapotecs, and the possibility of Mixtec presence there has yet to be documented archaeologically.

Mixteca Alta

Red-on-cream pottery is common, and distinctive varieties are known from the Nochixtlán Valley and the Coixtlahuaca Valley, possibly corresponding to Mixtec and Chocho speakers, respectively. The Nochixtlán Valley, especially, was a major center of late Mixtec culture: other characteristic artifacts from that area include flaked-stone scrapers made with Yucuñudahui chert, large ceramic ladles with trough-like handles, small pottery braziers with a wheel-like disk surface, and tiny pots possibly used in blood-letting rituals.

Burials in seated position, placed in subsurface pits just large enough to accommodate a bundled corpse, are common in the Nochixtlán Valley. Pit burials are also common in the Tejupan and Coixtlahuaca Valleys, though here the pits are several times the size needed to accommodate the corpses.

Graphite-on-orange and graphite-on-red pottery is common in the Mixteca Alta, although the total range of its distribution is not known. Another Mixtec manifestation is small stone sculptures: heads of black basalt depicting Tlaloc, the Central Mexican rain god, found in Tilantongo and Tlaxiaco; dogs and coyotes carved in basalt found in Teposcolula, and round or oval stones with crudely indicated facial features from Coixtlahuaca.

Mixteca Baja

This region is poorly documented for the City-State stage, Red-on-cream pottery has been found at sites as far west as Silacayoapan. Graphite-on-orange pottery and pottery made in the Nochixtlán Valley have been found at some sites, but a distinctively Mixteca Baja complex of traits has yet to be defined for the City-State stage. Presence of stamped base or *fondo sellado* bowls (that is, with an embossed design on the interior of the base) relates this region to the Tehuacán Valley to the north.

Sierra Zapoteca

Regionally distinctive artifacts undoubtedly are to be found here but late sites have yet to be studied. Among the elements similar to those of Valley of Oaxaca style are gray ceramics, including two-tone bowls (with color differentiation intentionally produced by firing), and gray bowls with tripod supports bearing effigy eagle and serpent heads.

Mixe Region

This mountainous area is known to have many sites of the City-State stage but none has been formally studied and reported.

Cañada

Gray bowls with tripod supports and stamped interior bases are common in the Cuicatlán area; one variety has deer-hoof effigy supports. Also characteristic are beads made of steatite, a soft greenish-white stone. Drum-shaped cut stones about 30 to 40 centimeters in diameter were used as column bases.

Toward the Oaxaca-Puebla border, around Teotitlán de Flores Magón, distinctive pottery includes ceramics of porous paste with white slip, red-on-white, or orange-on-white decoration. The Teotitlán area may have been occupied by Mazatecs or Popolocas while the Cuicatecs lived farther south around Cuicatlán.

Isthmus

This is a complex area that was occupied by Chontal, Mixe, Huave, Zapotec, and Zoque groups at the time of the Conquest. Comparative studies have yet to be made to determine whether these groups can be recognized archaeologically and what their pre-Hispanic distribution was.

A stone figure from the Mixe region. A number of pre-Hispanic survivals still exist in this area, among them a system of calendrical reckoning apparently derived from the ancient calendar.

One of the best-known sites in the Isthmus region is Guiengola on a moun tain saddle overlooking the alluvial coastal plain a few kilometers inland from Tehuantepec along the Tehuantepec river. It was a Zapotec center and has palaces a ballcourt, and a temple-patio-altar complex that show some continuity with Urban stage Zapotec architectural patterns. A thick, high, defensive wall of stone surrounds a large part of the site. At Guiengola the Zapotec leader Cocijoeza with his own men and Mixtec allies successfully fought off Aztec armies sent by his father-in-law, the Aztec emperor Ahuitzotl, thus preventing an Aztec take-over of Isthmus city-states. The lack of accumulated debris suggests that Guiengola either had a relatively short permanent occupation or that it was occupied seasonally rather than throughout the year. The site of Cerro Padre López in what is now Tehuantepec may have been the center of a city-state there.

The area around Jalapa del Marqués at the confluence of the Tequisistlán and Tehuantepec rivers was another major focus of pre-Hispanic occupation in the Isthmus region. The extensive alluvial lands here are now mainly flooded by the Benito Juárez dam, but many large sites exist around the periphery of the dam. One interesting characteristic reported from Salina Cruz and Juchitán as well as from Jalapa del Marqués are human burials found in ceramic pots They usually seem to be multiple burials in large vessels, but the example from Jalapa del Marqués consists of long bones that had been severed when fresh apparently so the pieces could fit in a small pottery jar.

Mazatec Sierra

The Cueva de Tenango is the best documented site in the Mazatec region Since San José Tenango is near the geographic center of the region, ceramics from the cave may be taken as representative of the region.

Cueva de Tenango ceramics can be divided into several groups. Some dec orated luxury vessels are clearly imports; for example, vessels of Teotitlán Incised, which came from around Teotitlán in the Cañada, Chinantla polychrome from the Chinantla, and yellow pottery with black and brown linear decoration also from the Chinantla.

Another group includes vessels which are common in other regions of Oaxaca and which were apparently made in many places during City-State times Among these, for example, are gray hemispherical bowls. Plain, utilitarian vessels such as pots and pitchers form a third group; dozens were found in the cave and presumably were locally made. Finally, three kinds of decorated pottery, also found in abundance, apparently represent distinctive Mazatec cultural expressions One kind, Tenango polychrome, has buff-colored paste with red, black, and white painted decoration. Another kind is white-slipped ware with black and red decoration, and a third is red-slipped pottery with white painted decoration

Chinantla

In addition to polychrome pottery, yellow-paste ceramics, sometimes with black or brown linear decoration, are characteristic of the Chinantla. Subsurface pits in the form of a boot were used for simple burials. As in other areas, some high-status individuals were buried in tombs. Gold ornaments have been found in a number of late tombs in the Chinantec region. Caves were also used for burials

Some artifacts, including stone sculptures, are similar to things from the Central Mexico area and may reflect Aztec occupation or the periodic presence of merchants in the Chinantla on their way to the Maya region. These traders may also have obtained goods such as cotton, feathers, and other lowland products from the Chinantla for supplying the Aztec capital of Tenochtitlan. The site known as El Castillo in what is now Tuxtepec was a major center and apparently under Aztec control in late times.

An unexplored mound at Ayotzintepec in the Chinantla. It is composed mostly of earth and adobe, typical of sites in this region.

Coast

Tututepec, in the foothills overlooking the extensive, fertile floodplain of the Río Verde and the lagoons just inland from the Pacific Ocean, was among the most important coastal centers. It was apparently a Chatino center, conquered during the City-State stage by the Mixtec leader 8 Deer. The lower Río Verde coastal plain is one of the best agricultural areas in Oaxaca and was important in the production of cotton and cacao. In contrast to their success in other Mixtec regions, the Aztecs failed to conquer and extract tribute from the kingdom of Tututepec.

Much of the coast of Oaxaca west of the Isthmus of Tehuantepec is rugged, dry and with few exceptions lacks extensive alluvial areas. During City-State times many settlements along the coast consisted of villages or hamlets with dispersed households. In some areas people may have exploited shellfish for making purple dye perhaps as a part-time activity supplementing agriculture.

The Lower Río Verde Valley was an exception to these coastal patterns. A wide floodplain and lagoon-estuary system made this a favorable area for pre-Hispanic occupation. Chatino and Mixtec groups probably lived here but whether their occupations can be distinguished from each other archaeologically has not been determined.

The Coast region also includes the picturesque bays now popular as resorts —Huatulco, Puerto Angel, and Puerto Escondido. Many small sites were located along the Coast in the late 1960s, and during the 1980s site survey and salvage excavations were carried out in the Huatulco area in connection with development of tourist facilities. Although the beaches are beautiful and marine resources such as turtles, lobster, oysters, and fish abound in the rocky coves, the relative scarcity of prime agricultural land and fresh water meant that these were marginal areas in pre-Hispanic times. In other words, they were distant from major centers of political and economic activity, had low population densities, and played only peripheral roles in social and cultural change.

Archaeological remains detected thus far around the coastal bays date from the City-State stage and reflect the same kind of extensive occupation by scattered homesteads that existed in other parts of Oaxaca. Some sites are right on the bays, and shells and fish bones in refuse attest to the use of marine resources.

According to historical documents, in late pre-Hispanic times the city-state of Tututepec dominated the Coast as far east as Huatulco, an area that includes the present towns of Puerto Angel and Puerto Escondido. The inhabitants of this large domain paid tribute in goods and services to the Mixtec lord c Tututepec.

Despite their marginal nature, these areas pose interesting questions fo archaeological study. What ethnic and linguistic groups occupied these smal settlements? Chatino, Chontal, and Zapotec are all possibilities, And where di they come from? Were specialized products—salt, dried fish, purple dye—involve in tribute, and could they have been the reason for colonizing these areas in th first place? Was there competition between the city-states of Tututepec an the city-states of the Isthmus for control of these areas? What earlier occupation took place along the Coast, and where did these groups originate? Since mos archaeological study in Oaxaca has focused on major centers of development particularly in the highlands, study of the small coastal sites could add nev dimensions to the archaeological record.

Oaxaca's languages and cultures were never more rich and divers than at the time of the Conquest. Populations expanded greatly durin the City-State stage and even isolated, marginal areas were colonized Political relations of the elite linked groups in different areas, so th complementary trends of diversity and unity were in full play.

The legacy of this rich and diverse past lives on in the 16 distinc ethnic and linguistic groups present today in Oaxaca. Future studie utilizing historical documents, linguistics, physical anthropology, an material remains will continue to elucidate and enrich Oaxaca's archaeo logical record and our understanding and appreciation of this comple: past.

The Conquest is exemplified at Mitla, in the Church Group, where more recen buildings are superimposed on the pre-Hispanic structures.

SITE DESCRIPTIONS

Several archaeological sites in the Valley of Oaxaca and in the Mixteca are open to visitors. Valley of Oaxaca sites are all within easy driving distance of Oaxaca City. Huajuapan de León, on Highway 190 three hours by car northwest of Oaxaca City, is a good base from which to visit Mixteca sites. Huajuapan has several hotels and restaurants. Guiengola, a mountaintop site on the Isthmus of Tehuantepec, is about five hours southeast from Oaxaca City.

Monte Albán, Mitla, and the Oaxaca Regional Museum are the three principal archaeological points of interest in Oaxaca that everyone should see. The visitor should allow a minimum of two hours to see Monte Albán. San José Mogote and Zaachila are both about half an hour by car from Oaxaca City and can be scheduled with Monte Albán to make nearly a full day's tour. A visit to Zaachila might also include a stop at the 16th-century Dominican monastery at Cuilapan.

In the Santo Domingo Church compound, the Oaxaca Regional Museum (closed Mondays), under the auspices of the INAH, displays artifacts found in archaeological excavations in Oaxaca, including such outstanding pieces as the original jewels, carved animal bones, and other artifacts from Monte Albán's Tomb 7.

The Tlacolula Valley sites—Dainzú, Lambityeco, Yagul, and Mitla—can be combined in another one-day trip which should also include the Frissell Museum in Mitla. The enthusiastic visitor might also want to schedule stops at Teotitlán del Valle where woolen rugs are made and sold, Santa Ana del Valle to see the local museum with pre-Hispanic and historical artifacts, Tlacochahuaya to see the colonial church, and the 2,000-year-old Tule tree next to the highway. The Sunday market at Tlacolula is another worthwhile attraction.

In contrast to the Valley of Oaxaca sites, the Mixteca sites—with the exception of Cerro de las Minas—are less fully explored and lack permanent INAH guards. Nevertheless, they may be of interest to the specialist or intrepid tourist. Some have small museums under the jurisdiction of the local community. Other points of interest in the Mixteca are the 16th-century Dominican monasteries at Coixtlahuaca, Teposcolula, and Yanhuitlán, and the market at Tlaxiaco. Access to the Mixteca sites can be difficult due to weather conditions and bad roads; facilities such as bathrooms and refreshment stands are not available. Visitors should also be aware that local people are under no obligation to provide services or assistance to outsiders.

According to Mexican federal law it is illegal to buy or sell artifacts, to pick up artifacts (including potsherds and other small items) on the surface of sites, or to undertake excavations without proper permits. Artifact-hawkers at sites like Monte Albán and Mitla mainly sell fakes, although they sometimes try to convince visitors that they have genuine pieces. Purchase of genuine pieces, no matter what size or quality, is prohibited by law.

Site descriptions which follow are presented in alphabetical order. See inside back cover for chronological chart.

Cerro de las Minas

This small urban center is built on a rocky hill at the north end of the Huajuapan Valley. Monumental stone-masonry structures cover the top of the hill and residential areas are spaced over the slopes. Large-scale excavations to open the site for visitors began in 1987.

The hill is shaped like a narrow ridge oriented northwest-southeast with rocky outcrops at each end. During Early Urban times (Ñudée phase, 500 B.C.-A.D. 100) the area between the outcrops was filled in and leveled. The two rock protrusions were modified with stone masonry construction and a third structure (Mound 2) was built. The top of the ridge took on a defensive character as vertical walls were added to the natural terraces, especially on the relatively gentle west slope.

Around A.D. 300-750 (Ñuiñe phase) Cerro de las Minas again became an important center. Earlier monumental constructions were renovated, and new stone facades, stairs, and exterior walls were added. A ballcourt was constructed on the west side of the site just below the top of the hill.

During the Ñuiñe phase a distinctive style of architecture, glyphs, and ceramic urns appeared in the Mixteca Baja at Cerro de las Minas and other sites, as described in the Urban stage chapter.

An archaeological museum, currently planned for Huajuapan, will exhibit materials found at Cerro de las Minas.

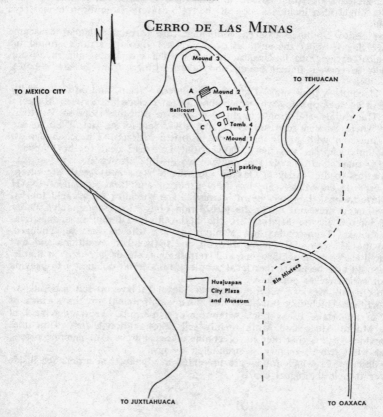

Of special interest at Dainzú is the tomb with lintel carved in the form of a jaguar with its forelegs and paws extending down along the door jambs. It has been suggested it might be a composite creature — head of a vampire bat and jaguar extremities.

Dainzú

Dainzú is located on a west-facing hillside next to a major tributary stream that originates in the mountains to the north, passes by the towns of Teotitlán del Valle, Macuilxochitl, Tlacochahuaya, and Abasolo, and then joins the Río Salado. Many archaeological sites are found along this tributary including a San José phase village at Abasolo. Intensive cultivation of the large expanse of alluvium immediately downslope from Dainzú would have provided food for the pre-Hispanic community. Dainzú, which means "hill of the organ cactus" in Zapotec, is unusual among large Valley of Oaxaca Urban stage sites in that it has no view of Monte Albán. Excavations were carried out in the 1960s.

The earliest documented occupation at Dainzú is an Early Rosario phase (700-600 B.C.) village. The main occupation, however, corresponds to Early Urban times when Dainzú was a town of some 1,000 inhabitants, and functioned as a second-level economic, political, and ceremonial center. Large-scale architectural works probably began in Period I, continued in Period II, and culminated in the period known as Transition II-IIIa (approximately A.D. 250-350) in the Monte Albán chronological sequence.

Highlights of the excavated portion of the site include Building A, a large platform constructed against the hillside and incorporating (on the south side of its lower wall) about 35 carved stone monuments, most of which depict ballplayers. They may have been carved in Late Period I or Period II as they appear to be re-used. Downslope to the west a complicated series of structures is exposed, including portions of patios, temples, and stairways. The architectural layout of the site is not clear since most structures were rebuilt and modified in pre-Hispanic times or are incompletely excavated.

The ballcourt at Dainzú has a playing field oriented east-west. The north half of the ballcourt is unexcavated; the south half shows construction of small, step-like stone blocks that would have been covered by stucco to form a sloping surface. The same construction technique was used in the main ballcourt at Monte Albán. The Dainzú ballcourt is presumably contemporaneous with the carved representations of ballplayers.

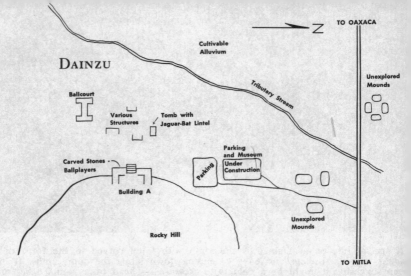

Dainzú may have been abandoned just before Period IIIa but human occupation continued in the area. Several large mounds next to the highway near the turn-off to Dainzú form the center of a Period IIIb-IV site. And, according to documentary evidence, Macuilxochitl, the town immediately to the north, was the principal town of a Period V city-state.

A visitors' center and museum to house the carved stones is under construction at Dainzú.

Diquiyú

Diquiyú is an unexcavated urban center on a high ridge top about 30 km. by air south of Cerro de las Minas. It overlooks the Huajuapan Valley to the north and the Santa María Tindú area to the south. The center of the site consists of large walls, platforms, and stairways extending some 500 to 700 meters along a ridge top. Erosion has removed part of the walls around the site center, but a monolithic corner some four meters high is still standing at the southeast corner of the main platform.

Several carved stones have been found at Diquiyú and residences occur on terraced slopes. An arroyo at the base of the mountain was probably the dry season water source for the inhabitants. The site appears to be an exception to the general association of urban centers with large expanses of fertile land since no such area is immediately evident.

Diquiyú — the name means "on top of stones" (diqui - atop; yu - stone) — is a little over an hour from Huajuapan on an unimproved dirt road. The site has not been uncovered for viewing.

Guiengola

Guiengola ("large rock" in Zapotec) is a mountaintop site on the southern Isthmus of Tehuantepec overlooking the alluvial plain of the Pacific Ocean. Immediately below the site to the east is the Río Tehuantepec, the only water source evident in the area.

The site is composed of stone buildings, including a palace and dispersed residences plus a site center with two high platforms and a ballcourt. A defensive wall, varying from two to three meters high and over a meter thick, surroun

104

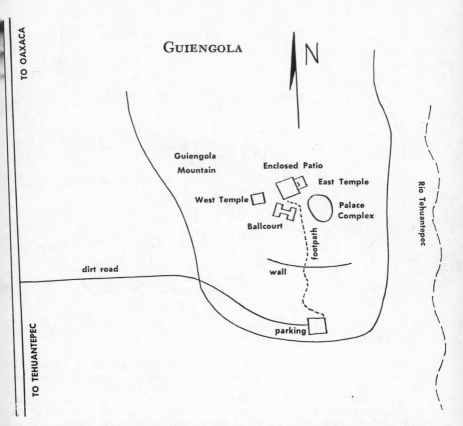

GUIENGOLA

TO OAXACA

TO TEHUANTEPEC

Rio Tehuantepec

Guiengola Mountain

Enclosed Patio

East Temple

West Temple

Palace Complex

Ballcourt

footpath

dirt road

wall

parking

the site. Preservation is remarkable, due in part to the dry climate, and many buildings are standing as in pre-Hispanic times. The construction, based on stone slabs with mud mortar, is delicate, however, and vandals and careless visitors have caused some damage by climbing on the walls. Stucco plaster is still in place on some walls.

Guiengola evidently served, during the City-State stage, as a place of refuge for Zapotec rulers and their followers who probably lived in Tehuantepec. The dry, rocky, inhospitable environment at Guiengola would have made permanent occupation difficult, although water and cultivable land were available at the base of the mountain.

The site is under INAH custodianship. A dirt road, usually in bad repair, goes part way up the mountain, and then one must walk about an hour to get to the site. This site is not recommended for the casual visitor.

Huamelulpan

This small urban center was occupied from about **400** B.C. to A.D. **600**. The site consists of five groups of construction, each on a separate ridge around the center of the present-day town of San Martín Huamelulpan. The largest group, behind the church, includes platforms, mounds, and a ballcourt. Several carved stones from the site are incorporated into the church walls.

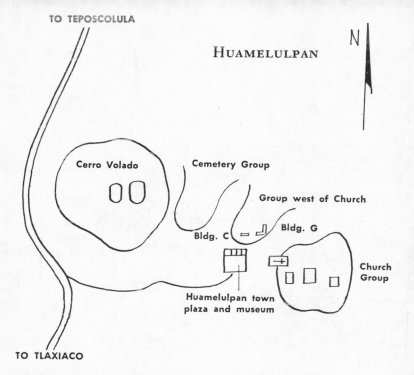

Building C is a platform with a corner of large monoliths. Calendric glyphs, apparently representing day signs, and a lizard are carved on the mono liths. Another platform, Building G, is also partially exposed.

The geographic situation of this site is intriguing. A small stream run through the present-day town but areas of alluvium are on the other side of th hill toward the north, out of view of the site and a couple of kilometers away

Excavations were carried out at Huamelulpan in 1957, 1961, and 1974, ex posing only small sections of the platforms. A local museum at Huamelulpa houses artifacts found at the site. Of special interest are several carved stone and ceramic urns.

Huijazoo or Cerro de la Campana

Cerro de la Campana, sometimes known as Huijazoo, is a large hillto site on lands of the municipalities of Huitzo and Suchilquitongo in the Etl. Valley. Founded in Period I, it became a major center in Period IIIb-IV. Th site is strung out along several adjoining ridges, with large structures clustere on ridge tops and residential terraces on the slopes below. The site was partiall explored during several seasons in the 1980s.

Tomb 5, discovered in 1985, is the largest and most elegant Urban stag Zapotec tomb known in Oaxaca. It is literally a house of the dead constructe in the same architectural format as Period IIIb-IV Valley Zapotec residence with a patio surrounded by rooms. The tomb has a huge stucco sculpture over th entrance, polychrome wall murals, exquisitely carved stone door jambs, and carved slab depicting members of a ruling family. Tomb 5 lies several meters below a long unexcavated mound on the north side of a large flat rectangula area; this complex is probably a palace. Immediately to the west are a ballcour

d two temple-patio-altar compounds which, together with the palace, comprise
e elite focus of the site.

This site was a major center of Zapotec art and symbolism as indicated by
mb 5 as well as many other Period IIIb-IV carved stones found there. Many
the carvings are made on the relatively soft pink volcanic tuff found on the
l which is still used today in Suchilquitongo for making tombstones.

The local name of the site is Cerro de la Campana. Archaeologist Enrique
éndez, who explored the site, called it Huijazoo. Fray Burgoa in his *Geográfica*
scripcion refers to Huijazoo when discussing the attempts of the Aztecs under
octezuma to penetrate Zapotec territory. Burgoa describes Huijazoo (which he
ys means "fortress" in Zapotec) as part of a great mountain range running
rth-south. It is doubtful that Cerro de la Campana is the place mentioned
Burgoa.

The site was abandoned after Period IIIb-IV. Some Late Period V sherds
ve been found on the surface but as yet no evidence of construction. The hill-
may have served temporarily as a fortress or refuge during City-State times
people living in Huitzo and Suchilquitongo. Both towns did have important
riod V occupations. A Period V tomb with 78 vessels was salvaged at Suchil-
itongo and an elite tomb containing gold and jade beads and polychrome
ttery was discovered in the Barrio del Rosario, Huitzo. The latter, known as
iitzo Tomb 1, has reused carved stones placed as door jambs and has been
t exposed for visitors.

Neither the site of Cerro de la Campana nor Tomb 5 are open to visitors.
restoration program to protect the Tomb 5 murals and sculptures is underway,
is a project to make copies of the paintings and carved jambs. A local museum
the town of Suchilquitongo displays photographs of Tomb 5 and artifacts
und in it.

he right jamb of the carved
one doorway to the main
amber of Tomb 5 at Cerro
la Campana. Each of the
o panels shows jaws-of-sky
top, then glyphs possibly in-
:ating personal names, then
personage shown in profile
inding facing left toward the
orway, as in a procession
ossibly honoring the deceased.
ich personage wears an elab-
ate feathered headdress and
rries a bag or offering.

Mound 190 at Lambityeco with stucco masks of Cocijo, the Zapotec Rain Go

Lambityeco

Lambityeco, excavated in the 1960s, is part of a large site called Yegu ("small hill" in Zapotec) which includes more than 200 mounds and was occupie continuously from at least as early as the Rosario phase, around 700 B.C. Th two main structures exposed at Lambityeco, Mound 190 and Mound 195, for part of the center of the Period IIIb-IV occupation dated from the time of th site's apogee between A.D. 600 - 750. Mound 195 includes a temple-patio-alta compound with two high-status residences joined to its east side. Stuccoed portra heads above the entrance to Tomb 6 and stucco friezes along the east edge o the patio of the Tomb 6 residence depict male and female leaders of the elit family.

Mound 190, immediately to the south, is another elite residence highlighte on the west side of the patio by an altar with two large stucco masks representin, Cocijo, the Zapotec rain god.

Lambityeco was important as a salt-producing site in Period IIIb-IV. Salt bearing ground water was boiled and evaporated in large ceramic jars producin, a residue of salt used locally and perhaps exchanged to Monte Albán and othe sites. The name "Lambityeco" apparently derives from the Spanish *alambiqu* which means "still," and evidently refers to the ovens where water was boile to produce salt. *Pityec* means "mounds" in Zapotec, so Lambityeco means "dis tillery mounds."

Like other large IIIb-IV communities, Lambityeco was a center of artisti expression as manifested in the elegant ceramic urns found in various contexts and in the carved bones and painted murals found in Tomb 11. (Tomb 11 is i an unexcavated mound on the north side of the highway.)

Lambityeco is under INAH custodianship. A few artifacts from the site including some fragments of the painted murals from Tomb 11, are on displa in the guards' quarters.

Mitla

Human occupation around Mitla is as early as anywhere in Oaxaca. Rock-shelters in the hills north of the town and sites near the river attest to human presence during the Lithic stage, several thousand years before Christ. Village and Urban stage occupations occur within the limits of the present-day town, and sometime after A.D. 750 Mitla became the principal town of one of the most important city-states in the Valley of Oaxaca. The name Mitla comes from the Nahuatl *Mictlan* meaning place of the dead (*Lyobaa* in Zapotec). Mitla was supposedly venerated as the place where the souls of the dead came to rest.

Five main pre-Hispanic architectural complexes are preserved within the center of the present-day town. Common households of this period were dispersed

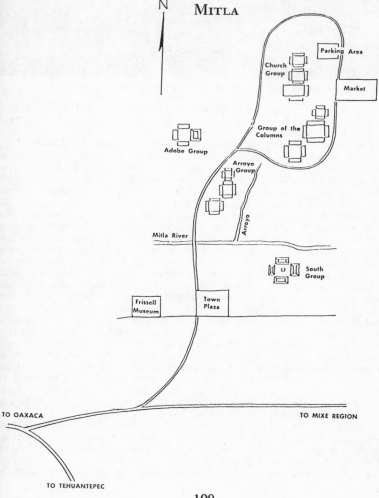

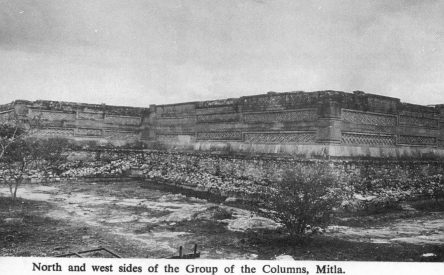

North and west sides of the Group of the Columns, Mitla.

on the hill slopes within a radius of several kilometers around Mitla, and fortress stands on a hill two kilometers to the west. The population was perhap between 2,000 and 5,000 people.

Two of the main building complexes, the *Adobe Group* and the *South Group* appear to be temple-patio-altar compounds similar to those at Monte Albán Both Mitla examples include a high mound on the east side with the patio t the west, like the TPA at Lambityeco. They may have been built and used durin the Urban stage and then continued in use during the City-State stage. Presum ably they functioned as ritual and ceremonial precincts.

The other three architectural complexes, the *Group of Columns, th Church Group,* and the *Arroyo Group,* were constructed in the City-State stag or Period V. Architecturally they are similar among themselves and probably ha residential and administrative functions. Each is composed of three patios partl or entirely surrounded by rooms. In each case the north patio is small, has re stricted access, and was apparently the residential patio. The relatively large middle patio is, in two cases, open to the south. The third patio—also large an sometimes open on one side—is not necessarily aligned with the others bu placed off to the southwest suggesting that it was a later and somewhat les integrated addition. The basic unit, then, is the residence connected to a possible administrative patio, plus a third, perhaps also administrative, patio. Size an elegance of construction suggest that the three complexes were occupied an controlled by elite families. The Group of the Columns, known for its mag nificent panels decorated with striking designs (grecas) of cut, mosaic stone is evidently the principal complex and may have been occupied by the suprem ruler or ruling family at Mitla. The others may have been occupied by high ranking nobles. Alternatively, these three complexes may have been built and occupied at slightly different times within the City-State stage.

The stone used for Mitla's buildings is volcanic tuff. Pre-Hispanic quarrie have been found at the base of the cliffs a few kilometers north of town. Stone was cut and shaped with harder stone tools by chipping, hammering, and abrad ing. Small mosaic grecas were placed in panels on the buildings as a decorative veneer over a core of adobe, mud, and rubble. Many of the geometric patterns

110

formed by the grecas are pan-Mesoamerican design elements. Large cylindrical columns in the Group of the Columns functioned as supports for wooden roof beams. Pre-Hispanic roof construction was something like the reconstructed example in the room on the west side of the interior patio of the Group of the Columns.

The Mitla church was constructed on top of and actually partly within the southernmost patio of the Church Group; stones from the latter were incorporated into the walls. Panels above the doors in the interior patio of the Church Group contained codex-style paintings; a few fragments are still visible.

In Patio F of the Group of the Columns a medium-size cruciform tomb was built beneath the north room and a huge, greca-paneled cruciform tomb below the east room. (A similar greca-paneled tomb occurs in analogous position in a patio of a residence at Xaaga, about 4.5 km. east of Mitla, which must have been the home of another elite family.) The Mitla tombs occur in administrative rather than residential patios and are of a size that could accommodate many more individuals than just immediate family members. Perhaps they were intended for nobles allied with or related to the principal ruler of Mitla.

At least some of the buildings at Mitla were in use at the time of the Conquest, and were subsequently abandoned, falling into disrepair. Various projects beginning around the turn of the century have been devoted to restoring and protecting the site, although the buildings never required the extensive exploration of most archaeological sites.

INAH custodians are on duty at Mitla. The two principal areas of the site —the Group of the Columns and the Church Group—can be seen in about an hour. The market next to the parking area offers a variety of handicrafts, especially clothing and other woven goods, many of which are produced in Mitla.

The Frissell Museum, just east of the Mitla town plaza, under the auspices of the University of the Americas - Mexico City, houses an outstanding collection of pre-Hispanic artifacts from Oaxaca, particularly ceramic vessels, urns, and carved stones.

Monte Albán

Monte Albán, Oaxaca's largest and most spectacular archaeological site, covers a cluster of low mountains in the center of the Valley of Oaxaca. It was by far the largest urban center in ancient Oaxaca and is the only one that has been extensively excavated. Even so, only a small portion, probably less than **one** percent of the total site, has been uncovered.

The pre-Hispanic and indigenous names for Monte Albán have not been preserved. "Monte Albán" is a European name perhaps derived from an early landowner or given to the mountain because it looked similar to a place in Italy.

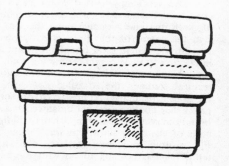

Stone model of a tomb facade found at Monte Albán. Note *doble escapulario* over entrance. Drawing after Paul Gendrop.

Exploration and consolidation of the stairway on the east side of Mound III on top of the South Platform at Monte Albán. Mound III is the highest point in the southern part of Monte Albán. The stone slab showing the person with the leaf, pictured on page 33, was found here. Excavations were first started on the South Platform in 1988; the major portion remains to be explored.

Explorations began at Monte Albán in the past century but most of the extensive work of excavation and reconstruction was done in the 1930s and 1940s, turning the site into a tourist attraction.

The ancient capital of the Zapotecs, Monte Albán was occupied for more than 1,200 years from 500 B.C. to A. D. 750. Monte Albán's chronological sequence applies to the entire Valley of Oaxaca and is divided into Periods I, II, IIIa and IIIb-IV, from early to late, with some subdivisions. The city was founded in Period I and abandoned in the Period known as IIIb-IV. (Period V in the Valley of Oaxaca sequence refers to a time after the abandonment of Monte Albán.) Monte Albán's largest structures are designated by letters (Building M, Building X, etc.), the highest building at each of the cardinal directions is designated with a Roman numeral.

At its height in Period III Monte Albán covered about 6.5 square kilometers including the outlying residential areas and the civic and ceremonial complexes of El Gallo and Atzompa on nearby hilltops. Maximum population is estimated at 25,000 to 30,000 inhabitants.

El Gallo and Cerro Atzompa, two hills northwest of Monte Albán with archaeological remains, are considered part of greater Monte Albán. These extensions of the main site began in Period I and reached their maximum growth in Period III. Neither hill has been extensively explored or opened for visitors.

The artificially-leveled Main Plaza at Monte Albán was the heart of the city. It is delimited by the gigantic North and South Platforms, and by rows of platforms and mounds along the east and west sides. Buildings G, H, I, and J in the center of the Plaza cover protruding bedrock outcrops.

Monte Albán's earthquake-resistant buildings are typically wide at the base in relation to their height. Some are built over bedrock outcrops and most include several stages of enlargement and rebuilding. A characteristic decorative architectural element, the so-called *doble escapulario* (a cornice in two planes with rectilinear pendants) is preserved on some buildings, often above a rectangular panel that contained stone or stucco bas-relief figures. The doble escapulario has been reconstructed on many of the buildings around the Main Plaza, partly on the basis of examples shown on small stone models of buildings found at the site.

Visitors frequently ask why the steps on Monte Albán's buildings are so tall. This has nothing to do with the size of the people; they were of approx

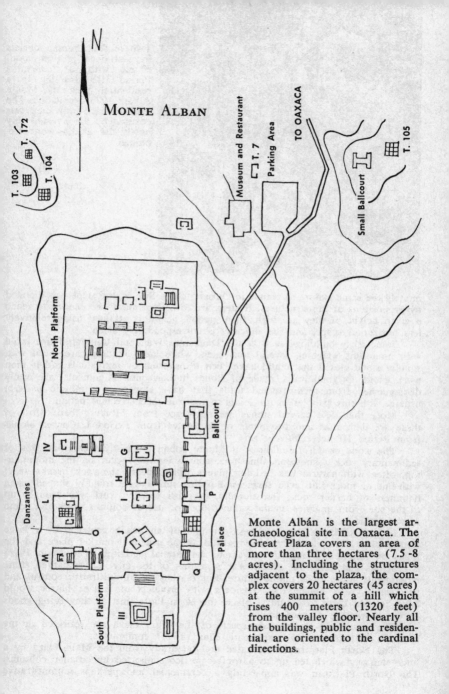

Monte Albán is the largest archaeological site in Oaxaca. The Great Plaza covers an area of more than three hectares (7.5 -8 acres). Including the structures adjacent to the plaza, the complex covers 20 hectares (45 acres) at the summit of a hill which rises 400 meters (1320 feet) from the valley floor. Nearly all the buildings, public and residential, are oriented to the cardinal directions.

113

Two of four human buri; in slab-lined graves ass ciated with a low-stat Period IIIb dwelling in residential area of Mon Albán; 1973 excavation. T head of each individual w covered by an inverted cl bowl; the skulls were tr phined.

imately the same stature as people in Oaxaca today. Size of the steps was dictate by proportions of the structures. If steps are low, then many are needed to read a given height; if they are high, then greater height is attained using relative less horizontal space, and the stairway is correspondingly steep.

Some early buildings such as the Danzantes Wall and Building J are face with monoliths weighing several tons each, while later buildings are faced wi smaller stone blocks that could have been transported by individuals rather tha work gangs. Original walls, made of stones in horizontal alignments, are easi distinguished from reconstructed walls that have stones in a mosaic pattern usually with tiny pebbles in the joints to indicate recent reconstruction.

More than 550 carved stones are registered from Monte Albán. Most c these are danzantes and fragments of danzantes from Period I. Carved stone from Period III are relatively rare.

The stone used for buildings at Monte Albán is mostly local; outcrops o sedimentary rock (sandstone, limestone, conglomerates) occur on the mountain top, often with natural flat bedding planes which means the rock breaks apar with one or more flat, even surfaces. Building stones were roughly shaped usin hammers of harder rock. Occasionally, greenish volcanic tuff was brought u to the site from quarries on the valley floor for use as column bases and som carved stelae.

Monte Albán is Oaxaca's best example of an urban center with a larg central plaza. The plaza must have served as the principal market place and th focus of community administrative and ceremonial activities. The Main Plaza is spacious and accessible from various sectors of the city. Large carved stone monuments attest to its public nature. For reasons of administrative control and practicality, it is logical that outsiders with products to sell or barter would have brought them to a central place, the Main Plaza, just as they bring goods to the market in Oaxaca today.

The ritual and ceremonial aspects of the Main Plaza are reflected in the presence of temples and temple-patio-altar (TPA) compounds.

The North Platform is separated architecturally from the Main Plaza by a huge stairway which led up to a roofed portico supported by circular columns. The North Platform was apparently a ceremonial and perhaps administrative ea of relatively restricted access. The South Platform may also have served remonial functions and at least in Period IIIb-IV had a TPA on top of it.

Monumental structures and residential zones cover the ridge tops and slopes tending out from the Main Plaza. Residential areas were probably divided to neighborhoods with local temples and perhaps administrative buildings and arkets.

Residences and temples at Monte Albán are easily differentiated by their chitectural layout. Residences have narrow doorways and rooms around a uare patio. Temples have wide doorways and one or two rectangular rooms. mbs and burials are usually found in association with residences. High-status riod III residences include "The Palace" on the east side of the Main Plaza, d the residences of Tombs 104 and 105. Tomb 172, a medium-size tomb with nes and ceramic offerings still in place, is associated with a medium-size resi- nce. Tomb 125 has painted door jambs and is also associated with a medium- ze residence. Smaller residences lack tombs but have slab-lined graves beneath e room floors. No examples are exposed for viewing.

Burials with trephined skulls have been found in association with some small sidences. Monte Albán may be unique in Mesoamerica as a place where tre- nination was practiced. Holes were drilled or cut in the skull while individuals ere alive; presumably this was done with some sort of anesthetic and for edical reasons, though precise motives remain unknown.

Natural springs in the barrancas and on the hillsides would have supplied onte Albán's early inhabitants with water. However, these sources would have minished as the population grew and the mountain was deforested. During the iny season (May through October) water for domestic use could have been llected using drains and in-house patios. Despite the presence of a large stern in the Main Plaza (used in Period II and later filled in) and a Period III servoir on the northwest edge of the site, water must have been scarce during e dry season (November-April) and probably had to be carried up to the te from wells in the alluvium or from the river at the base of the mountain.

Many tunnels and passageways exist at Monte Albán. Some were exploratory enches made by archaeologists to study the sequence of construction. These n be distinguished by their flat roofs made of concrete slabs. Other tunnels e original and may have served as drains, passageways, or both. One example the passageway through the point of Building J. The roof, made with stone abs in inverted V-shape, is incomplete. Two low tunnels go from the west d east sides of the cistern in the center of the east side of the Main Plaza out d up to Buildings H and II. These must have served as passageways rather an drains, since the low parts would have filled with water.

The Sunken Patio on the North Platform is drained by a subterranean pas- geway that emerges on the west side of the main North Platform stairway. nother passageway-drain led out of the Main Plaza underneath the South latform.

A minimum of two hours is needed to see Monte Albán, and the visit should clude at least a walk around the Main Plaza. At the south end one can see xamples of carved stones and buildings from Period I (Building L and the anzantes Wall), Period II (Building J and the "conquest slabs"), and Period III the South Platform and the carved stelae at its northeast and northwest corners). he top of the South Platform provides a magnificent panoramic view of the alley of Oaxaca, as do the buildings atop the North Platform. A visit to Tomb 04 allows one to see a tomb in the context of a residence as well as some of e accompanying high-status elements such as the urn above the tomb entrance, carved door slab, and the polychrome wall paintings.

Under INAH custodianship, Monte Albán has a visitors' center with museum, bathrooms, restaurant, and shops. The museum houses some of the most important carved stones from the site, protecting them from gradual deterioration brought about by exposure to sun, rain, and wind. Replicas of these stones are placed in the site.

Monte Negro and Tilantongo

Tilantongo is a dispersed Mixtec community. The town center and Colonial church are located on an archaeological site which had an Urban stage occupation and was especially important during the City-State stage as the political capital of the famous Mixtec ruler 8 Deer. This archaeological site has been tested but not uncovered for viewing.

Monte Negro is an Early Urban stage archaeological site on a mountain about a two-hour walk, mostly uphill, from the center of Tilantongo. Several buildings made of cut limestone blocks were excavated and consolidated in the 1930s and are visible today. The site was once considered older than Monte Albán, though we now know that it was contemporaneous with Late Period I and Period II at Monte Albán. The site is more than a square kilometer in extent and includes a central area with temples and high-status residences, some aligned along a street running east-west. Residences also occur on terraces downslope. The temples are low platforms with cylindrical columns to support the roof. Residences near the site center are of closed format, that is, rooms around a patio. Tombs are simple and rectangular in shape.

Stone platform at the Early Urban center of Monte Negro. Blocks of hard, buff colored limestone quarried on the mountaintop served for walls and foundations. Platforms, temples and residences at Monte Negro are similar in architectural layout to those at the contemporaneous site of Yucuita.

The occupation at Monte Negro corresponds to the Ramos phase (500 B.C. to A.D. 250). Pottery, architecture, and burial customs are similar to those documented at Yucuita. The hill of Yucuita, some 30 km. to the north, is visible from Monte Negro, and the two sites evidently flourished at the same time.

A small local museum at Tilantongo next to the municipal offices is open sometimes; on display are archaeological pieces from the area.

San José Mogote

San José Mogote, centrally located in the Etla Valley and surrounded by first-class agricultural land, was always an important place in pre-Hispanic Oaxaca. During the Village stage it was the largest and probably the most important community in the Valley of Oaxaca. The occupation began by 1400 B.C. and perhaps earlier. Relatively elaborate and well-preserved Tierras Largas phase residences were partially excavated on the west edge of the site. Some had adobe walls about one meter high, and apparently consisted of patios surrounded by rooms. This would be the earliest evidence in Oaxaca so far for the closed house layout. One of these, sometimes claimed to represent a "public building," is exposed for viewing.

The site was particularly important during the Olmec horizon (1200-850 B.C.) when there was a population of several hundred inhabitants. Workshops for making magnetite and shell ornaments were present, as well as some unusually skilled pottery makers. Etlatongo in the Nochixtlán Valley of the Mixteca Alta is the only other site known in Oaxaca where such elegant and varied pottery with Olmec-style designs has been found.

At the end of the Village stage, in the Late Rosario phase, there was some status differentiation at San José Mogote, and the beginning of large-scale construction was probably underway. The precocity of San José Mogote in

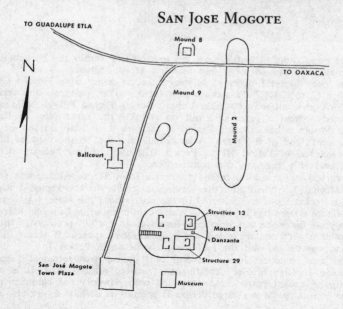

SAN JOSE MOGOTE

117

Monument 3 from San José Mogote depicts a danzante reminiscent of those from Monte Albán; probably of Late Monte Albán I date. It shows a standing figure with a trilobal swirling glyph on his chest, perhaps representing sacrifice, and a calendrical date 1L (Alfonso Caso's Glyph L), possibly the person's name. An arrow-and-dot motif, known also from the Mixteca Alta and elsewhere in the Valley of Oaxaca in Early Urban times, is shown twice curving around the edge of the stone. Monument 3 may have originally been placed vertically at the corner of a platform, and was later removed and reused in the fill between two structures. The symbols and dates accompanying the danzantes are among the earliest writing in Mesoamerica.

terms of population size may have led to conflicts within the community; one group may have moved away and founded Monte Albán.

San José Mogote functioned as a second-level center from Periods I through III (500 B.C. to A.D. 750) serving as a local market, political, and ceremonial center for communities in the Etla Valley. During Period I large buildings were constructed around a plaza laid out on roughly the same plan as the Main Plaza at Monte Albán. During Period II temples were built on top of Mound 1 at the south end of the plaza. A large ballcourt just to the west of the plaza was constructed in Period III; a Period IIIa tomb, found beneath the stucco floor, presumably predates the construction.

A carved stone, similar to the danzantes from Monte Albán, was found on top of Mound 1. Stylistically, the carving is similar to the Period I danzantes, and Late Period I pottery occurred in the area where the stone was found. The carved figure covers one broad surface and continues around on one narrow side. This suggests the stone was originally displayed in upright position in the corner of a building with one wide and one narrow face exposed. It seems likely that the stone was carved and the building constructed in Period I.

The local museum houses several outstanding archaeological pieces. One is a Period I effigy brazier depicting the face of an old man. It is made of white-slipped, cream pottery and decorated with powdery red cinnabar pigment. Another unusual piece is a large Period II greenstone or jade figure also partially vered with red cinnabar. These two pieces were found in association with uctures atop Mound 1.

A distinctive type of Period II gray ceramic urn is known from San José ogote. These urns show personages with Cocijo masks; they make use of flat ces of pottery to form the headdress and decorative elements. Traces of red d yellow paint are often preserved. Some examples from different excavations the site are on display in the local museum and others, evidently looted from e site, are in the Frissell Museum in Mitla.

agul

The archaeological site of Yagul is on an island of volcanic tuff surrounded highly productive alluvial land; to the south is the Río Salado and to the rth is a major tributary that originates in the mountains behind the site. agul was first occupied during the Urban stage, beginning in Period I. In Period an arrowhead-shaped building was constructed at Caballito Blanco on a sep- ate bluff about one km. south of Yagul. In Period IIIb-IV residences and obably civic and ceremonial structures were built at Yagul.

Yagul was especially important in the City-State stage and most of the uctures now visible were constructed then. The site is also known as *Pueblo ejo* and was apparently the forerunner of the present-day town of Tlacolula. agul" means "old tree" in Zapotec.

Explorations were carried out at Yagul in the late 1950s and the early 60s; buildings were exposed and consolidated and the site was opened for sitors. Construction stone at Yagul consists mainly of river cobbles of volcanic cks such as basalt. Similar stone was also used at Lambityeco and Dainzú. oximity to Mitla (about 10 km. as the crow flies) implies some interaction it the size and elegance of Yagul's structures—palaces, ballcourt, possible cer- nonial precinct, and fortress—all suggest that Yagul was an autonomous city- ate. Grecas formed with a mosaic of small cut stones link Yagul with Mitla terms of architectural decoration. The *Palace of the Six Patios,* also known pularly as the Labyrinth because of the intricate passageways and many rooms, tually consists of three complexes, each formed by two patios surrounded by oms. The northernmost patio of each pair has relatively limited access and as probably a residence; the southernmost patio, sometimes open on one side, more accessible and may have functioned as an administrative area for the ouse. The same architectural layout is present at Mitla.

Patio 1, the ample space immediately southeast of the Palace of the Six atios is delineated by rooms on the west, north, and possibly the east sides. mple size and openness suggest this was administrative rather than residential ace, perhaps analogous to the large patios of the Group of the Columns and e Arroyo Group in Mitla.

South of **Patio 1** is a temple with the same architectural layout as Urban age temples. If built in City-State times, it would exemplify long continuity in apotec architectural patterns.

The ballcourt, in characteristic I shape with the playing field oriented east- est, was presumably constructed in City-State times.

Patio 4, immediately southeast of the ballcourt, appears to be a temple- atio-altar compound (TPA) formed by four mounds with an altar in the center. ne highest mound is on the east side, as is the case with the TPA at Lambityeco ystem 195) and the two TPAs (the Adobe Group and the South Group) at itla. Yagul's TPA may have been built during the Urban stage (Period IIIb-IV) d continued in use with modifications of the structures in the City-State stage eriod V). A frog-effigy boulder sculpture is visible at the base of the east

119

Partial view of structures at Yagul with the Palace of the Six Patios above right. Patio 1 is at center rear. At the left is the ballcourt; far left, part of TPA complex.

mound. Tomb 30, below the center of the patio, is Period V; it has three chamber and panels decorated with grecas.

The fortress on the bluff above the site center is naturally defensible; mo of its perimeter is defined by sheer cliffs though in some places rock walls we built to add protection and limit access.

A Period IIIb-IV residential area is present on a terrace northwest of th excavated buildings. Low-status Period V residences were presumably disperse on terraces and slopes surrounding the main site area in a pattern similar other late pre-Hispanic sites.

INAH custodians are on duty at Yagul. The visitor should allow about a hour to walk around the site.

Visible here in the restored walls of the Palace of Six Patios are river cobble commonly used in ancient construction at Yagul.

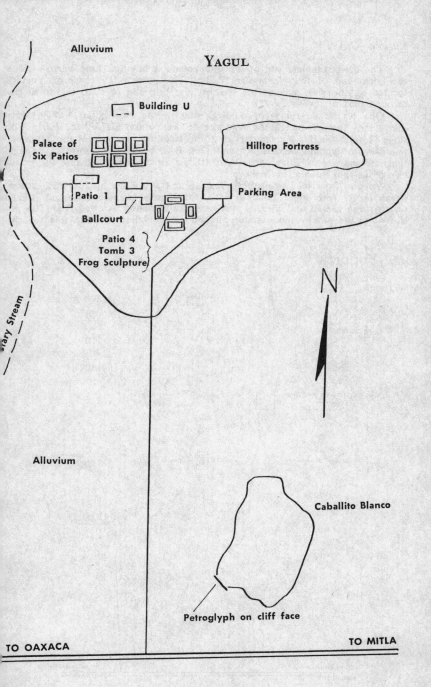

Yagul

Alluvium

Building U

Palace of
Six Patios

Hilltop Fortress

Patio 1

Ballcourt

Parking Area

Patio 4
Tomb 3
Frog Sculpture

...ary Stream

N

Alluvium

Caballito Blanco

Petroglyph on cliff face

TO OAXACA

TO MITLA

Yucuita

The archaeological site of Yucuita covers a hill and long narrow ridge
the north end of the Nochixtlán Valley. The present-day town of Yucuita
located on the west side of the base of the hill; the road to the town pass
through part of the site.

One of the largest archaeological sites in the Nochixtlán Valley, Yucui
had a long though interrupted sequence of occupation. During the Early Villa
stage (1500 1200 B.C.) it covered 20-30 hectares and was one of the largest cor
munities in highland Oaxaca. Around 1200 B.C. Yucuita lost most of its popul
tion and the site of Etlatongo, about 10 km. to the south, became the princip
village in the Nochixtlán Valley.

Yucuita flourished again beginning around 500 B.C.; by 200 B.C. it was a
urban center with some 2,000 to 3,000 inhabitants. Sometime around A.D. 1(
construction ceased and Yucuita was largely abandoned. Around A.D. 300 pow
shifted to the nearby mountaintop site of Yucuñudahui; Yucuita was reoccupi

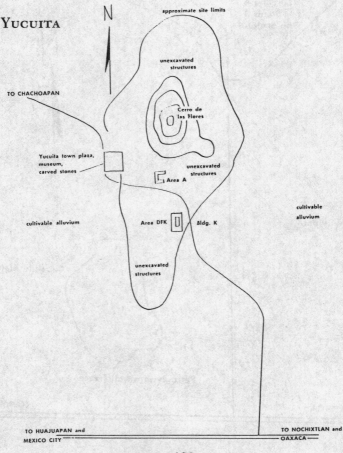

functioned as a second-level center. Although inhabited into the Colonial iod, Yucuita never again was the main settlement in the valley. The archaeoical site includes a conical hill known by its Mixtec name, Yucuita (*yucu*-hill, flower), and a long, flat hill extending out from it like a peninsula to the th. The entire site is almost surrounded by cultivable alluvial lands, with main expanse next to the river to the west. Huge stone walls about five ters high delimit the east side of the site and blocked access to the site center. rge platforms, drainage systems with tunnels, and elite residences occur on the peninsula. Small residences of dependent families are found on the site skirts. Several satellite communities are situated one to three kilometers from main site. Each has a high-status or elite residence and several lower-status, endent households.

Two areas of the Early Urban stage settlement are excavated and conidated. Area A is a high-status residence. Area DFK is a large platform with drain, and an unfinished monumental stairway.

A small museum in the center of the town next to the municipal office ises ceramics and other artifacts recovered in excavations at the site; and eral carved stones are set up in the town plaza.

cuñudahui

Yucuñudahui (*yucu*- hill; *ñdahui* - mist, in Mixtec) is a major Late Urban ge center on a mountaintop, about four km. north of Yucuita and overlooking Nochixtlán Valley from the north. Large stone-masonry buildings occur ng the ridge tops and include a ballcourt, platforms, and two large tombs. ooden roof beams are still preserved in Tomb 1. Residential terraces are found the slopes, particularly the south-facing slope toward Yucuita.

Outcrops of high-quality chert at Yucuñudahui were exploited from at least rly Urban times on, and during the City-State stage there were extensive rkshops for production of teardrop-shaped scrapers used in production of lque, a beverage made by scraping out a cavity in the heart of a maguey plant, noving the sap as it collects, and allowing it to ferment. These scrapers were tributed widely throughout the Nochixtlán Valley.

On the slopes above the town of Chachoapan along one of the paths up to acuñudahui is Iglesia Vieja, a second-level center of the City-State stage. high-status residence at this site was partially excavated by Michael Lind.

Yucuñudahui is on lands of the towns of Santa María Chachoapan and San ateo Coyotepec. The site, an hour's walk above the towns, should be visited th authorization of town officials.

achila

Zaachila is an extensive archaeological site within the town of the same me. Much of the site is buried beneath the Río Atoyac alluvium, though me mounds and platforms rise above the floodplain. The center of the site, st north of the town plaza, is built on a huge rock outcrop that protrudes from e alluvium like an island. This area was occupied from at least Early Urban nes (a possible Village stage occupation remains to be documented), and er became the center of a major city-state. According to documentary evidence, achila was the principal town of the Late Period V Zapotec city-state ruled Cocijoeza.

Roughly half of the site center is preserved. The northern and western porns were partly destroyed, beginning with construction of the church in the

123

sixteenth century. House lots and streets continue to affect the site peripheries although the central area is protected as an archaeological zone.

In 1962 archaeologist Roberto Gallegos cleared off the patio of a residence and found Tombs 1 and 2 beneath the floor. Both tombs contained elaborate offerings of polychrome pottery, gold ornaments, and carved bones. Tomb has motifs sculpted in stucco on the walls. This treasure is similar to and roughly contemporaneous with the contents of Monte Albán's Tomb 7 and reflects the wealth and importance of the ruling family or families of Zaachila during City-State times.

The Zaachila tombs are also contemporary with the large cruciform tombs of Mitla and Xaaga. Architecturally, however, the Zaachila tombs resemble high-status Period III tombs at Monte Albán, such as Tombs 103 and 104, rather than the Mitla and Xaaga tombs. Why? Perhaps the Zaachila tombs were constructed in Period IIIb-IV and then reused in Period V. If the Zaachila and Mitla-Xaaga tombs were constructed at the same time, then they represent two distinct late architectural styles in the Valley of Oaxaca.

There is another bedrock island with adobe construction in the Barrio San Sebastian a few blocks east of the town plaza. Tombs 3 and 4 were discovered here beneath the floor of a chapel built over the mound. Though less elaborate than Tombs 1 and 2, they, too, contained bones and offerings of the City-State stage.

The main site is open to visitors and under INAH custodianship.

ZAACHILA

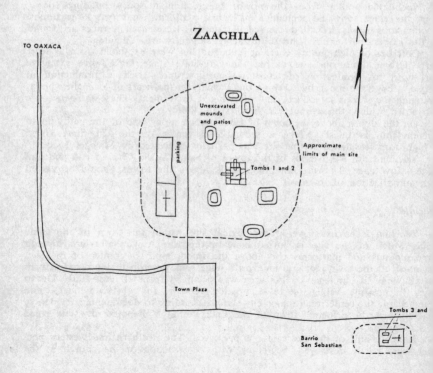

TO OAXACA

Unexcavated mounds and patios

parking

Approximate limits of main site

Tombs 1 and 2

Town Plaza

Tombs 3 and

Barrio San Sebastian